Working With
The
Mental Health Act

Second Edition

Written by

Steven Richards *BA (Hons)* & Aasya F Mughal *LLB (Hons), Barrister*

First edition September 2006

Second edition September 2008 published by

Matrix Training Associates
2 The Green
North Waltham
Hampshire RG25 2BQ

www.matrixtrainingassociates.com

Data supplied by

British Library Cataloguing in Publication Data
A catalogue record for this book is available from the British Library

ISBN 978 0 9552349 2 7

Printed and bound in England

Working With The Mental Health Act

CONTENTS

Working With The Mental Health Act

The Mental Health Act provides the authority to detain and treat people with a mental disorder in hospital. It also allows for the supervision of people in the community. It is a substantial and sometimes complex piece of legislation. The Mental Health Act (herein referred to as the 'Act') is arranged like a book and is divided into chapters called Parts. Each Part contains numbered paragraphs called sections. The expression that a person has been 'sectioned' actually means they are subject to the powers of a numbered paragraph of the legislation. Altogether, there are 149 separate sections, not all of them allow for detention. Each section relates to different powers and rules governing the operation of the legislation.

The sections of the Act that specifically provide the power to detain a person vary in several ways including:

- their duration – from 6 hours to many years
- the professionals involved, for example – nurse, doctor, police officer, approved mental health professional
- treatment – whether a person can be given treatment without their consent
- discharge – who can discharge the person
- appeals – the person's right of appeal against detention

The powers of the Mental Health Act are considerable as they override two basic rights. Usually, a person can only be detained if they have committed an offence. Under the legislation however, a person is detained not because of a crime but because they have a mental disorder that needs hospital treatment. The other basic right is that an adult with mental capacity to consent can only be given treatment with their consent. Again, the Act overrides this and makes psychiatry unique in the medical profession for authorising treatment that can override the refusal of consent by an adult with capacity.

Mental Health Act 2007

The Mental Health Act 2007 made a number of important amendments to the original Mental Health Act 1983, although large parts of the 1983 Act were unchanged. This book provides a guide to the Mental Health Act 1983 as amended by the Mental Health Act 2007. The majority of changes made by the 2007 Act came into force on 3rd November 2008. The amendments are incorporated throughout the book into each chapter. Consequently this book is accurate as of 3rd November 2008 unless stated otherwise in the text. Some of the most significant changes are summarised below.

New Rights

- *Advocacy*

The right to advocacy for the majority of detained patients was introduced. This service is to be provided by advocates known as independent mental health advocates (IMHAs). They provide support and information to detained patients about their rights. In England the service is not due to start until April 2009 although the Welsh service will start earlier (see page 124).

- *Nearest Relative*

Patients were given the right to displace their own nearest relative. A further reason to displace a nearest relative was added, that the nearest relative is *'unsuitable to act'*. In addition, civil partners were given the same status as married partners within the Act when deciding a person's nearest relative (see page 116).

- *16 – 17 year olds*

A young person with capacity to consent or refuse admission to hospital is now able to do this without the person with parental responsibility for them (usually parents) being able to override their decision (see page 137).

- *Electro-convulsive therapy (ECT)*

New rights for patients to refuse ECT were introduced (see page 82).

New Powers

- *Community Treatment Orders (CTOs)*

A community power (also called Supervised Community Treatment) replaced the previous community power called Supervised Discharge. Special rules apply for people on supervised discharge prior to November 2008. They will need to be assessed for possible transfer to a community treatment order (see page 39).

- *Deprivation of Liberty Safeguards (DOLS)*

The power to detain people who lack capacity in their best interests in order to prevent harm to them. The Mental Health Act 2007 was used as the vehicle to introduce this power although it is formally part of the Mental Capacity Act 2005. The power does not come into force until at least April 2009. For further details email: dols@dh.gsi.gov.uk.

Website: *www.dh.gov.uk/en/SocialCare/Deliveringadultsocialcare/MentalCapacity/ MentalCapacityActDeprivationofLibertySafeguards/index.htm*

Improved Protection

- *Mental Health Review Tribunal/Panel (MHRT)*

The duties placed upon hospitals to refer a patient's case to the Tribunal were increased (see page 100).

- *Young people under 18*

Under 18s were given improved protection in a number of areas. The time limits for automatic referrals to the Mental Health Review Tribunal were reduced (see page 100). Further, where a person under 18 is admitted to hospital (voluntarily or detained), the managers of that hospital must take particular action (see page 137). If a person under 18 is being considered for ECT (whether detained or not) special rules apply (see page 82). The treatment of those under 16 subject to community treatment orders is also covered by special rules (see page 85).

- *Criminal offence*

The original criminal offence in the Act of ill-treatment or wilful neglect of a person with a mental disorder remains but the maximum term of imprisonment for a person found guilty of this offence was increased from two to five years (see page 128).

People

- *Approved Mental Health Professionals (AMHP)*

Replacing the position of the approved social worker (ASW) an approved mental health professional may be a nurse, social worker, occupational therapist or psychologist. Their role is primarily the same as the approved social worker they replaced, to assess people for detention under the Act (see page 120).

- *Approved Clinicians and Responsible Clinicians (AC and RC)*

The role of the responsible medical officer (RMO) previously undertaken by consultant psychiatrists, has been replaced by that of approved clinicians and responsible clinicians. These new positions can be filled by nurses, occupational therapists, social workers, psychologists and doctors (see page 122).

Working With The Mental Health Act

Change in detention criteria

- *Definition of mental disorder*

The four previous categories of mental disorder (mental disorder, severe mental impairment, mental impairment, psychopathic disorder) were replaced by the single term 'mental disorder'. Mental disorder is defined as any disorder or disability of the mind (see page 154).

- *Appropriate treatment*

In order to detain a patient under a long-term section, appropriate treatment must now be available (see page 79).

- *Exclusions*

The conditions previously excluded from detention (promiscuity, other immoral conduct or sexual deviancy) were removed as it is accepted that these are not mental disorders and therefore to specifically exclude them from the detention criteria is unnecessary. However, dependency on alcohol or drugs remains specifically excluded (see page 154).

- *The meaning of treatment*

The requirement that treatment should alleviate or prevent a deterioration of the patient's condition in cases of mental impairment and psychopathic disorder was removed from the explicit detention criteria. However a similar definition now applies for *any* mental disorder (see page 79).

Miscellaneous

- *Duty on hospitals to inform victims*

If a person is detained under Section 37, 47 or 48 after committing an offence of a sexual or violent nature, the detaining hospital has a duty to inform the victims of the offence when certain decisions are being made in relation to the section.

- *Conflicts of interest*

New rules on conflicts of interest when applying the Act were introduced (see page 127).

- *Restriction orders*

From 1st October 2007, all new forensic restricted sections were made with no expiry date (without limit of time).

- *Section 135(1) and 136 transfer*

From 30th April 2008 the ability to transfer people between different places of safety whilst on Section 135(1) or 136 was introduced (see page 109).

Transition period

The changes to: the criteria of mental disorder; the requirement that appropriate treatment is available; and the treatability test do not affect those people detained under the Act before 3rd November 2008. They remain detained as before and do not need re-assessment due to the changes. However, when renewal or discharge is being considered, the changes brought in by the Mental Health Act 2007 should be applied. For further details see:

www.dh.gov.uk/en/Publicationsandstatistics/Publications/PublicationsPolicyAndGuidance/ DH_086566

Further information

Further sources of information on the 2007 Act are given on page 145.

The 2007 Act placed a requirement on the Secretary of State to include a number of principles in the Code of Practice to the Act. The principles provide guidance when making decisions under the Act. Staff are under a legal duty to 'have regard' to the guidance given in the Code, including the principles. A new Code, reflecting the changes made by the 2007 Act, was published in August 2008 (see page 115).

The principles are:

> *'Purpose principle*
>
> *Decisions under the Act must be taken with a view to minimising the undesirable effects of mental disorder by maximising the safety and well-being (mental and physical) of patients, promoting their recovery and protecting other people from harm.*

> *Least restriction principle*
>
> *People taking action without a patient's consent must attempt to keep to a minimum the restrictions they impose on the patient's liberty, having regard to the purpose for which the restrictions are imposed.*

> *Respect principle*
>
> *People taking decisions under the Act must recognise and respect the diverse needs, values and circumstances of each patient, including their race, religion, culture, gender, age, sexual orientation and any disability. They must consider the patient's views, wishes and feelings (whether expressed at the time or in advance), so far as they are reasonably ascertainable, and follow those wishes wherever practicable and consistent with the purpose of the decision. There must be no unlawful discrimination.*

> *Participation principle*
>
> *Patients must be given the opportunity to be involved, as far as is practicable in the circumstances, in planning, developing and reviewing their own treatment and care to help ensure that it is delivered in a way that is as appropriate and effective for them as possible. The involvement of carers, family members and other people who have an interest in the patient's welfare should be encouraged (unless there are particular reasons to the contrary) and their views taken seriously.*

> *Effectiveness, efficiency and equity principle*
>
> *People taking decisions under the Act must seek to use the resources available to them and to patients in the most effective, efficient and equitable way, to meet the needs of patients and achieve the purpose for which the decision was taken.'*

On any one day there are, on average, 15,300 people detained in hospitals under the Act across England and Wales [1]. The proportion of detained patients on wards has increased in recent years according to the annual census of in-patients. In 2005, approximately 39% of mental health in-patients were detained and in 2007, the figure was 43% [1]. For the year ending March 2007 the number of detentions under the Act was 48,000 [2].

Protection from liability

Sections 64I and 139 of the Act provide staff with protection from civil or criminal liability for the actions they take when using the legislative powers to physically detain and forcibly treat people. This protection is only available if the Act has been used properly and does not apply if the actions in question were done in bad faith or without reasonable care.

Rights

People detained under the Act are given legal rights, the most prominent of which is the right of appeal to the Mental Health Review Tribunal and the Hospital Managers. The Tribunal is an independent judicial body that has the power to discharge detained patients. In addition, the Mental Health Act Commission/Care Quality Commission has an independent role to monitor the use of the legislation and the care of people detained under it.

Limitations

Whilst the powers of the Act are considerable, the legislation is limited in its application. To be detained a person has to meet certain legal criteria, all of which are designed to reduce the number of people affected by the legislation. The Act is largely confined to in-patient settings and treatment can only be given for mental disorder. Being placed on a section does not mean staff can take control of finances or make any other treatment decisions without consent.

Age range of the Act

The Act does not have a lower or upper age limit except in the case of guardianship. However, certain parts of the Act do contain special rules when the person is under 18. For younger people under 18, the legislation overlaps with the Children Act and other legislation and, in such cases, services should choose the most appropriate legislation (see page 137).

Where is the Act effective?

The Act is effective in, and its powers limited to, England and Wales.

Note

This guide provides a detailed explanation of the Mental Health Act, however it should not be regarded as a substitute for the Act itself. Nothing in it is intended to be, or should be, relied upon as legal advice. If you have any comments on the content or suggestions for future editions please email: *books@matrixtrainingassociates.com*.

- **Definition of mental disorder** – the Act is limited in its use to people who have a mental disorder which is defined in the legislation as '*any disorder or disability of the mind*' (see page 154).

- **Powers to admit and treat people in hospital** – over 20 different sections provide the powers to detain a person for assessment and/or treatment of a mental disorder. Each section differs in relation to a number of matters including the maximum detention period allowed, the professionals required, the appeal procedures and the treatment regulations.

- **Criminal and court related powers** – a series of sections that allow courts and prisons to transfer people from the criminal justice system to hospital for assessment and treatment of mental disorder.

- **Community powers** – guardianship and community treatment orders provide the means to deliver supervised care in the community for certain people (see page 34).

- **Treatment** – the power to override a detained person's wishes and give them treatment for mental disorder without their consent. The legislation provides a number of mechanisms to safeguard this power and limit its use (see page 79).

- **Mental Health Review Tribunal** – the independent judicial body to which many patients can appeal against detention. The Tribunal has the power to discharge the patient from detention at the end of a hearing if, based on the evidence they have heard and read, they are satisfied the patient does not meet the detention criteria within the Act (see page 100).

- **Hospital Managers** – under the Act, the Hospital Managers represent the NHS Trust (or other body) that formally detains a person. They have a number of duties under the legislation including holding appeal hearings for patients. They also have the power to discharge patients from section following the hearing (see page 104).

- **Independent Mental Health Advocacy** – the right to advocacy for the majority of detained patients. Provided by independent and specially qualified advocates (see page 124).

- **Mental Health Act Commission/Care Quality Commission** – the official body that monitors the use of the legislation and makes regular visits to review the care and treatment of detained patients. The Commission also provides guidance and information on the legislation (see page 113).

- **Nearest relative** – an important part of the Act that formally assigns a nearest relative to a detained person and gives that relative authority within the legislation (see page 116).

- **Code of Practice** – a statutory code concerning the practical use of the Act. It represents current thinking on best practice when using the legislation. Staff are under a legal duty to have 'regard' to the Code when using the Act (see page 115).

- **Conflicts of interest** – rules that protect from potential conflicts of interest in the use of the Act by staff and others (see page 127).

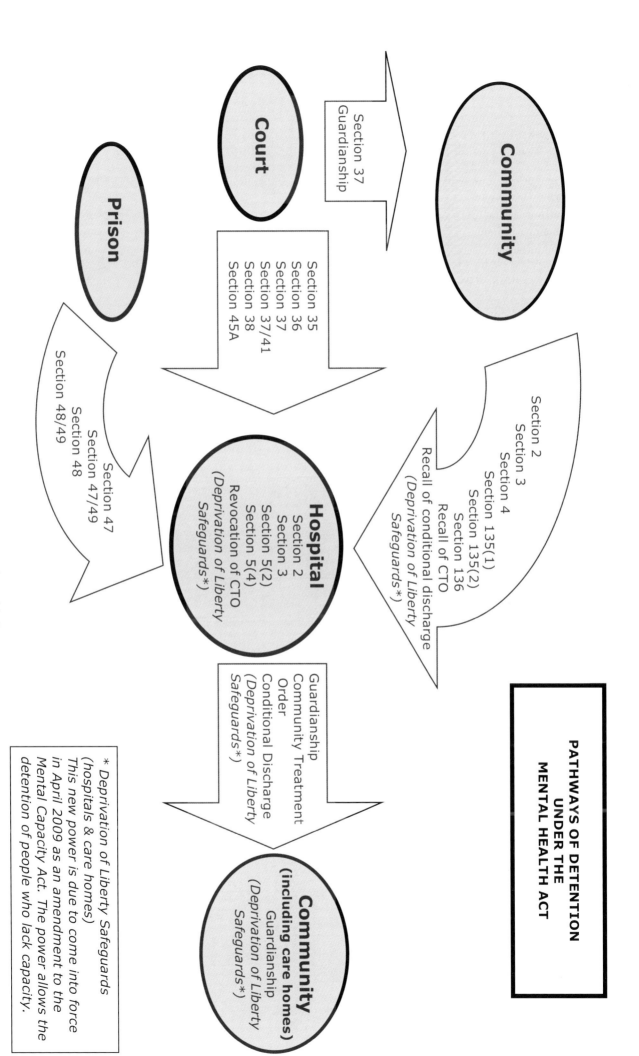

PATHWAYS OF DETENTION
UNDER THE
MENTAL HEALTH ACT

Community

Section 37
Guardianship

Court

Prison

Section 35
Section 36
Section 37
Section 37/41
Section 38
Section 45A

Section 2
Section 3
Section 4
Section 135(1)
Section 135(2)
Section 136
Recall of conditional discharge
Recall of CTO
(Deprivation of Liberty Safeguards*)

Section 47
Section 47/49
Section 48
Section 48/49

Hospital

Section 2
Section 3
Section 5(2)
Section 5(4)
Revocation of CTO
(Deprivation of Liberty Safeguards*)

Guardianship
Community Treatment
Order
Conditional Discharge
(Deprivation of Liberty Safeguards*)

**Community
(including care homes)**

Guardianship
(Deprivation of Liberty Safeguards*)

* *Deprivation of Liberty Safeguards (hospitals & care homes) This new power is due to come into force in April 2009 as an amendment to the Mental Capacity Act. The power allows the detention of people who lack capacity.*

The Act provides the powers to admit people living in the community to hospital by force. This becomes necessary when a person with a mental disorder needs hospital admission for assessment or treatment of their mental health and refuses voluntary admission or lacks capacity to consent to admission. The detention must be necessary for assessment, treatment or both. Eight different sections can be used and they differ in a number of ways. This chapter illustrates the power of each section and their practical application.

Sections 2 and 3 may also be used to detain a voluntary patient already in hospital who wishes to leave.

The periods of detention are set out below however, Section 3 and the Deprivation of Liberty Safeguards are renewable.

Section	Professionals required	Duration
Section 2	Two doctors and an approved mental health professional or nearest relative	up to 28 days
Section 3	Two doctors and an approved mental health professional or nearest relative	up to 6 months and renewable
Section 4	A doctor and an approved mental health professional or nearest relative	up to 72 hours
Section 135(1)	A magistrate, an approved mental health professional, a police officer and a doctor	up to 72 hours
Section 135(2)	A magistrate, a police officer and an authorised person	up to 72 hours
Section 136	A police officer	up to 72 hours
Recall of community treatment order (see page 39)	A responsible clinician	up to 72 hours
Recall of conditional discharge (see page 69)	A responsible clinician and the Ministry of Justice	the time limit (if there is one) of the restriction order

Deprivation of Liberty Safeguards (see page 130)	*This new power is due to come into force in April 2009 as an amendment to the Mental Capacity Act. The power allows the detention of people who lack capacity.*	*up to 12 months and renewable*

Note: The Act contains rules regarding conflicts of interest that those undertaking assessments to detain a person must follow (see page 127).

SECTION 2
ADMISSION FOR ASSESSMENT

Summary The power to detain and treat a person in hospital for up to 28 days. It is used for the assessment and treatment of people who have, or are believed to have, a mental disorder. There must be an intention to assess the person for this power to be used.

The section can be used in a number of ways: to forcibly admit a person from the community into hospital; to prevent a voluntary in-patient leaving hospital or to detain a patient for a longer period if they are already on a short-term section, such as Section 4, 5(2), 135(1) or 136.

Legal criteria

The person is suffering from *mental disorder*

and it is of a *nature or degree* to warrant detention in hospital for assessment or assessment followed by treatment for at least a limited period

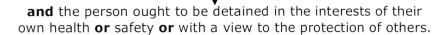

and the person ought to be detained in the interests of their own health **or** safety **or** with a view to the protection of others.

The words in italics are defined on page 154

Powers • *Detention* – the power to detain a person for up to 28 days in hospital.

• *Treatment* – the person can be given treatment for mental disorder with or without their consent (see page 79).

• *Absconding* – if the person absconds, they can be forcibly returned to hospital by any authorised member of hospital staff or by the police.

Who is involved? Two *doctors*, one of whom must be Section 12 approved (have experience of psychiatry) or be an approved clinician. In addition, if practicable, one doctor should already know the person or at least have some knowledge of the person **and** an *approved mental health professional* or *the nearest relative* (known as 'the applicant').

Each person can make separate recommendations for the section or they can undertake a joint assessment. Each must interview the patient and at least one doctor must discuss the case with the applicant.

The statutory forms require the doctors to give reasons why informal (voluntary) admission is inappropriate. The approved mental health professional must state that detention under Section 2 is the most appropriate way of providing the care and treatment the person needs. If neither doctor knew or had any knowledge of the person before making their recommendations, the approved mental health professional (or nearest relative) must explain why it was not possible to use a doctor who knew the person.

Time limits *Medical forms* – there must be no more than five days between the two medical examinations.

Working With The Mental Health Act

Application – the applicant (approved mental health professional or nearest relative) must have seen the person in the 14 days prior to making the application.

Admission – the person must be admitted to hospital within 14 days from the date of the last medical interview for the section.

Leave of absence	The responsible clinician can grant leave of absence (Section 17) for any period of time. However, as Section 2 is a short-term assessment power, prolonged leave would not be considered good practice.
Patient rights	Appeals The right of appeal to the Mental Health Review Tribunal within 14 days of the section commencing. The patient has one right of appeal to the Tribunal within the Section 2 detention period. The patient also has the right of appeal to the Hospital Managers at any time and without limit to the number of appeals, at the discretion of the Hospital Managers. Advocacy The right to an independent mental health advocate (IMHA). Mental Health Act Commission/Care Quality Commission The right to be visited by and complain to the Mental Health Act Commission/ Care Quality Commission.
Duties on staff	Staff should take all practicable steps to ensure the patient understands their legal rights and provide this information both orally and in writing (the Department of Health produces standard rights leaflets). If an approved mental health professional completes the section they are obliged, before or within a reasonable time after, to take such steps as are practicable to inform the person's nearest relative that a Section 2 is to be, or has been made and inform the nearest relative of their legal rights.
Discharge	There are a number of ways for the section to end: ❖ Discharge by the responsible clinician (RC) before the end of the 28 days ❖ Discharge by a Mental Health Review Tribunal ❖ Discharge by a Hospital Managers' hearing ❖ Discharge by the nearest relative ❖ Lapse of the Section 2 after 28 days. Allowing the section to expire through passage of time would not be considered good practice, as any detention should end as soon as the legal criteria no longer applies to the patient.
Renewing the section	Although Section 2 cannot itself be renewed, a person can be detained for a further period of time by the completion of a Section 3 before the Section 2 expires.
Forms	Form A1 - application by nearest relative **or** Form A2 – application by an approved mental health professional Form A3 or A4 - joint or single medical recommendations Form H3 - record of detention in hospital

Code of Practice	The Code states Section 2 should be used if '*the full extent of the nature and degree of a patient's condition is unclear; there is a need to carry out an initial in-patient assessment in order to formulate a treatment plan, or to reach a judgement about whether the patient will accept treatment on a voluntary basis following admission.*'
Facts	During the year ending March 2007, Section 2 was used 21,600 times[2], making it the second most used detention power after Section 3. Figures show that only 4,871 Section 2 orders were later changed to Section 3 orders indicating that the majority of patients detained under Section 2 were discharged or became informal patients rather than being detained further under Section 3.
Mental Health Act 2007	The following changes to Section 2 were introduced by the 2007 Act: <ul><li>The single definition of mental disorder</li><li>The introduction of approved mental health professionals</li><li>The introduction of approved and responsible clinicians</li><li>The right to an independent mental health advocate (IMHA)</li><li>Time under Section 2 included in the automatic referral period for Section 3 Tribunal referrals.</li></ul>

Summary   This section gives the power to detain and treat a person in hospital for up to six months. The power is renewable for further periods of time if required.

The section can be used in a number of ways: to forcibly admit a person from the community into hospital, to prevent a voluntary in-patient leaving hospital or to detain a patient for a longer period of time if they are already on a short-term section, such as Section 2, 4, 5(2), 135(1) or 136.

Legal criteria

The person is suffering from *mental disorder*

and it is of a *nature or degree* which makes it appropriate for them to receive medical treatment in hospital

and it is necessary for the health **or** safety of the person **or** for the protection of others that they receive that treatment

and treatment cannot be provided unless they are detained

and *appropriate medical treatment is available* for them.

The words in italics are defined on page 154

Powers

- *Detention* – the power to detain a person for up to 6 months initially.

- *Treatment* – the person can be given treatment for mental disorder with or without their consent (see page 79).

- *Absconding* – if the person absconds, they can be forcibly returned to hospital by any authorised member of hospital staff or by the police.

Who is involved?   Two *doctors,* one of whom must be Section 12 approved (have experience of psychiatry) or be an approved clinician. In addition, if practicable, one doctor should already know the person or at least have some knowledge of the person **and** an *approved mental health professional* or the *nearest relative* (known as 'the applicant').

Each person can make separate recommendations for the section or they can carry out a joint assessment. Each must interview the patient and at least one doctor must discuss the case with the applicant. If neither doctor knew or had any knowledge of the person before making their recommendations, the nearest relative or approved mental health professional must explain why. The approved mental health professional must state that detention in hospital is the most appropriate way of providing the care and treatment the person needs.

The doctors must give reasons why the stated mental disorder is of a nature or degree that makes it appropriate for treatment in hospital, and in addition why treatment can only be provided whilst the patient is subject to detention. They should further state why other options such as crisis response and home treatment or informal (voluntary) admission are not appropriate.

Working With The Mental Health Act

Time limits	*Medical forms* – there must be no more than five days between the two medical examinations.
	Application – the applicant (approved mental health professional or nearest relative) must have seen the person in the 14 days prior to making the application.
	Admission – the person must be admitted to hospital within 14 days from the date of the last medical interview for the Section 3.
Leave of absence	The responsible clinician may grant leave of absence (Section 17) for any period of time. However for the responsible clinician to grant any period of leave over seven consecutive days, they must first consider whether the patient could be placed on a community treatment order instead (see page 39).
Patient rights	Appeals The right of appeal to the Mental Health Review Tribunal once during each period of detention. The right of appeal to the Hospital Managers at any time and without limit to the number of appeals, at the discretion of the Hospital Managers. Advocacy The right to an independent mental health advocate (IMHA). Mental Health Act Commission/Care Quality Commission The right to be visited by and complain to the Mental Health Act Commission / Care Quality Commission.
Duties on staff	Informing the patient Staff should take all practicable steps to ensure the patient understands their legal rights and provide this information both orally and in writing (the Department of Health produces standard rights leaflets). Nearest Relative The approved mental health professional must consult the patient's nearest relative (unless such consultation is not reasonably practicable or would involve unreasonable delay) as part of their assessment. A nearest relative must be given enough information about the Section 3 application for detention and the reasons for it to allow them to form an opinion as to whether they want to oppose the application. If the nearest relative objects to the section, it cannot proceed. A section can then only be completed if the relative is displaced (removed) by a court (see page 116). Mental Health Review Tribunal If the person does not appeal to the Mental Health Review Tribunal six months after the start of the Section 3 (or the start of Section 2 if the person was detained under Section 2 immediately before the Section 3) the hospital must refer their case to the Tribunal for an appeal hearing. If the person has not had a Tribunal hearing for three years, their case must also be referred to the Tribunal. If the person is under 18, this three year period is reduced to only one year before their case must be referred to a Tribunal. Aftercare The provision of after-care services under Section 117 upon discharge (see page 111).

Discharge	There are a number of ways for the section to end:

❖ Discharge by the responsible clinician before the end of the six months

❖ Discharge by a Mental Health Review Tribunal

❖ Discharge by a Hospital Managers' hearing

❖ Discharge by the nearest relative

❖ Lapse of the section at the end of the detention period. Allowing the section to expire through passage of time would not be considered good practice as any detention should end as soon as the legal criteria no longer applies to the patient.

❖ Transfer (discharge) to a community treatment order

Renewing the section

The section can be renewed before it ends by the responsible clinician (Form H5). The renewal would allow detention for a further six month period. Subsequent renewals allow detention for periods of up to one year. The responsible clinician must examine the patient and the renewal must be agreed by another person professionally concerned with the patient's medical treatment. This second person must belong to a different profession to that of the responsible clinician.

Court rulings on renewals have stated that it is lawful to renew a Section 3 whilst the patient is on leave provided they are receiving, or are expected to receive, hospital treatment (the definition of which includes out-patient appointments and/or ward rounds) and that this treatment makes up a significant element of their care plan. The renewal criteria are very similar to the initial Section 3 detention criteria.

The legal criteria for renewal are:

The person is suffering from mental disorder

and the mental disorder is of a nature or degree which makes it appropriate for them to receive medical treatment in hospital

and it is necessary for the health **or** safety of the person **or** for the protection of others that they should receive such treatment

and it cannot be provided unless they continue to be detained

and appropriate medical treatment is available for them.

Forms

Form A5	- application by nearest relative **or**
Form A6	- application by an approved mental health professional
Form A7 or A8	- joint or single medical recommendations
Form H3	- record of detention in hospital

Code of Practice

'Section 3 should be used if: the patient is already detained under section 2 (detention under section 2 cannot be renewed by a new section 2 application); or the nature and current degree of the patient's mental disorder, the essential elements of the treatment plan to be followed and the likelihood of the patient accepting treatment on a voluntary basis are already established.'

Working With The Mental Health Act

'Compulsory admission should, in particular, be considered where a patient's current mental state, together with reliable evidence of past experience, indicates a strong likelihood that they will have a change of mind about informal admission, either before or after they are admitted, with a resulting risk to their health or safety or to the safety of other people.'

Case Law	An approved mental health professional cannot make a lawful application for detention under Section 3 if they are aware that the patient was recently discharged by a Mental Health Review Tribunal, unless they know of information which was not put before the Tribunal and this information makes a substantial difference to the case the Tribunal heard. *(From the case of R (on the application of von Bradenburg [2003])* If the adverse effects on the patient outweigh the benefit of the involvement of the nearest relative, it may be considered impracticable to consult with the nearest relative. Adverse effects can include factors such as a negative impact on their mental health, emotional or physical well-being, or leading to financial abuse. *(From the case of (R (on the application of E) v Bristol City Council [2005] EWHC 74, QBD)*
Facts	Section 3 is the most used detention power of the Act. For the year ending March 2007, it was used a total of 22,700 times[2].
Mental Health Act 2007	The 2007 Act introduced a number of changes to Section 3: • The single definition of mental disorder • The introduction of approved mental health professionals • The introduction of approved and responsible clinicians • The additional detention criteria that appropriate medical treatment must be available • The requirement that a second professional must agree before the section can be renewed • The ability to discharge the person subject to a community treatment order • The changes to the treatment powers • The right to an independent mental health advocate (IMHA) • Changes to the automatic referral periods for Tribunal hearings • To grant leave of absence over seven consecutive days, consideration must be given to the use of a community treatment order instead

SECTION 4
ADMISSION FOR ASSESSMENT IN CASES OF EMERGENCY

Summary The power to forcibly admit and detain a person in hospital for up to 72 hours. It may be applied when staff want to place a person under Section 2 (28 days) but are unable to get two doctors as required by Section 2 and the person needs urgent hospital admission.

Legal criteria

> It is of urgent necessity for the person to be admitted and detained under Section 2 of the Act (see the legal criteria for Section 2 on page 9)
>
> ↓
>
> **and** compliance with the requirements of Section 2 (two doctors and an approved mental health professional) would involve undesirable delay.

Powers

- *Admission and detention* – the power to admit someone forcibly from the community to hospital and detain them for up to 72 hours.

- *Treatment* – the power to treat a person forcibly under the Act does not apply to this section. Treatment could only be given if the person has capacity and consents or, if they lack capacity to consent to treatment, by using the powers of the Mental Capacity Act 2005.

- *Absconding* – if the person absconds they can be forcibly returned to hospital by any authorised member of hospital staff or by the police.

Who is involved? One *doctor,* if practicable they should already know or have some knowledge of the person **and**
an *approved mental health professional* or the *nearest relative* (known as the 'applicant').

The doctor must state that an emergency exists and give the number of hours delay it would cause to get a second doctor (to complete Section 2 instead) and that such delay might result in harm to the patient, those caring for them or other persons.

If the doctor did not know the person before making their recommendation, the approved mental health professional or nearest relative must explain why it was not possible to use a doctor who did know the person. The approved mental health professional must state that detention in hospital is the most appropriate way of providing the care and treatment the person needs.

Time limits *Application* – at the time of making the application, the approved mental health professional or nearest relative must have seen the person during the previous 24 hours.

Admission – the person must be admitted to hospital within 24 hours of either the doctor's examination *or* the approved mental health professional's *or* the nearest relative's application being made – whichever is earliest.

Detention – the 72 hour period of detention begins from the point at which the person is admitted to hospital.

Leave of absence Does not apply as Section 4 is a short-term section for assessment.

Patient rights	Appeals If a patient does appeal to the Mental Health Review Tribunal, it will take no action until they are informed that the Section 4 has become a Section 2 or 3 and they will then make arrangements for an appeal hearing. Advocacy No right to an independent mental health advocate (IMHA). Mental Health Act Commission/Care Quality Commission The right to be visited by and complain to the Mental Health Act Commission/ Care Quality Commission.
Duties on staff	Staff should take all practicable steps to ensure the patient understands their legal rights and provide this information both orally and in writing (the Department of Health produces standard rights leaflets).
Discharge	There are two ways for the section to end: ❖ If the assessment for Section 2 or 3 that takes place during the 72 hour period concludes that neither is required, the responsible clinician should discharge the section. ❖ The section expires after 72 hours. Allowing the section to expire through passage of time would not be considered good practice as the assessment for Section 2 or 3 should take place within the 72 hour period and determine the next step - either further detention or immediate discharge from the section.
Renewing the section	Section 4 cannot be renewed but it can be 'converted' to a Section 2 within the 72 hours with the addition of a second medical recommendation. If Section 3 is completed within the 72 hours it overrides the Section 4. The medical recommendation used in the original Section 4 cannot be used as one of the medical recommendations for the Section 3 and two new medical recommendations would be necessary.
Forms	Form A9 - application by nearest relative **or** Form A10 - application by an approved mental health professional Form A11 - medical recommendation for emergency admission Form H3 - record of detention in hospital
Code of Practice	*'Section 4 should be used only in a genuine emergency, where the patient's need for urgent assessment outweighs the desirability of waiting for a second doctor. To be satisfied that an emergency has arisen, the person making the application and the doctor making the supporting recommendation should have evidence of: an immediate and significant risk of mental or physical harm to the patient or to others; danger of serious harm to property; or a need for physical restraint...'*
Practical advice	When converting to a Section 2 from a Section 4, the two medical forms when taken together, must comply with the requirements of Section 2. The converted Section 2 will run from the date the person was admitted to hospital. An approved mental health professional (or nearest relative) does not have to be involved but they should be informed that the section has been converted.
Facts	For the year ending March 2007, there were 1,000 hospital admissions using Section 4. Of this figure, 25% were not detained for any further period of time[2].
Mental Health Act 2007	The 2007 Act made the following changes to Section 4: ▪ The introduction of approved mental health professionals ▪ The introduction of approved and responsible clinicians

Working With The Mental Health Act

SECTION 135(1)
WARRANT TO SEARCH FOR AND REMOVE A PERSON

Summary The power to forcibly enter a property to look for and remove a person to a place of safety (usually hospital) for assessment for a period of up to 72 hours.

Legal criteria

> It appears to a magistrate that there is reasonable cause to suspect that a person believed to be suffering from *mental disorder*
>
>
>
> has been, or is being, ill-treated, neglected or kept otherwise than under proper control
> **or**
> is living alone and unable to care for themselves.
>
> *The words in italics are defined on page 154*

Powers

- *Entry* – the power to forcibly enter locked premises, on one occasion only, to look for a person.

- *Removal* – the power to remove the person, if considered necessary, to a place of safety (usually hospital).

- *Detention* – the power to detain the person for up to 72 hours in a place of safety with a view to completing a Section 2 or 3. The person can be transferred to one or more other places of safety during the 72 hour period (for example from a police station to a hospital) (see page 109).

- *Treatment* – the power to treat a person forcibly under the Act does not apply to this section. Treatment could only be given if the person has capacity and consents or, if they lack capacity to consent to treatment, by using the powers of the Mental Capacity Act 2005.

- *Absconding* – if the person absconds they can be forcibly returned to hospital by any authorised member of hospital staff or by the police.

Who is involved? *An approved mental health professional* makes the application to a magistrate
and
a magistrate issues the Section 135(1) warrant
and
a police officer is authorised by the warrant to enter locked premises (by force if necessary) and remove the person.

The police officer must be accompanied by an approved mental health professional and a doctor (preferably Section 12 approved or approved clinician status).

Time limits *Warrant* – the warrant must be used within one month of being issued.

Detention – the 72 hour period of detention begins from the person's admission to the place of safety.

Leave of absence Does not apply as this is a short-term section for assessment.

Patient rights <u>Appeals</u>
No right of appeal to the Mental Health Review Tribunal.
No right of appeal to the Hospital Managers.

Advocacy
No right to an independent mental health advocate (IMHA).

Mental Health Act Commission/Care Quality Commission
The right to be visited by and complain to the Mental Health Act Commission/ Care Quality Commission.

Duties on staff	Staff should take all practicable steps to ensure the patient understands their legal rights and provide this information both orally and in writing (the Department of Health produces standard rights leaflets).
Discharge	There are two ways for the section to end:
	❖ Those making the assessment for Section 2 or 3 may decide that neither is appropriate.
	❖ The section automatically expires after the 72 hours. Allowing the section to expire through passage of time would not be considered good practice as the assessment for Section 2 or 3 should take place within the 72 hour period.
Renewing the section	Section 135(1) cannot be renewed but a person can be detained further by the completion of a Section 2 or 3 before the Section 135(1) ends.
Forms	The magistrate will issue a Section 135(1) warrant.
Practical advice	If the name of the person is unknown, the warrant will still be valid. However, it must state the premises to which it relates.
Code of Practice	*'Magistrates have to be satisfied that it is appropriate to issue a warrant. They are likely to ask applicants why they are applying for a warrant, whether reasonable attempts to enter without a warrant have been made and, if not, why not.'*
	If possible, once the police have gained entry, the accompanying approved mental health professional and doctor should carry out an initial assessment of the person with a view to considering whether any further assessments or any care and treatment will be necessary.
	Place of safety
	The preferred place of safety is hospital, however each area must decide on the most appropriate places of safety available to them and their use in different circumstances. A place of safety as defined in the Act is *'any police station, prison or remand centre, or any hospital the managers of which are willing temporarily to receive him'*. For young people under 18, a place of safety has the same meaning as in the Children and Young Persons Act 1933 where a 'place of safety' means a community home provided by a local authority or a controlled community home, police station, hospital, surgery, or any other suitable place, the occupier of which is willing temporarily to receive a child or young person.
	A police station should only be used as a place of safety in exceptional circumstances, for example, because the person's behaviour would pose high unmanageable risk to others if they were kept in a hospital.
Mental Health Act 2007	The 2007 Act made the following changes to Section 135(1):
	▪ The single definition of mental disorder
	▪ The ability to move a person from one place of safety to another.
	▪ The introduction of approved mental health professionals

SECTION 135(2)
WARRANT TO SEARCH FOR AND REMOVE A PATIENT

Summary The power to forcibly enter a property to look for and remove a detained patient who is absent without leave from hospital. If the person allows entry to the property voluntarily, there is no need to obtain a Section 135(2).

Legal criteria

On information given, it appears to a magistrate that

there is reasonable cause to believe that a patient already subject to a section is to be found on premises within the jurisdiction of the magistrate

and admission to the premises has already been refused or a refusal of such admission is predicted.

Powers
- *Entry* – the power to forcibly enter locked premises, on one occasion only, to look for the person.
- *Removal* – the power to remove the person if found on the premises and return them to the place they were previously detained.
- *Treatment* – once found, the power to treat the person under the powers of the original detaining section.
- *Detention* – once found, the person returns to hospital under the powers of the original detaining section.

Who is involved? An *authorised person* (for example from the NHS Trust) or a *police officer* who makes the application to a magistrate
and
a *magistrate* who issues the Section 135(2) warrant
and
a *police officer* who is authorised by the section to enter locked premises by force and remove the person. The police officer *may* be accompanied by a doctor or other authorised person from the hospital or local social services authority such as an approved mental health professional.

Time limits The warrant must be executed (used) within one month of being issued.

Leave of absence Does not apply as Section 135(2) is a short-term section.

Patient rights

Appeals
No right of appeal to the Mental Health Review Tribunal.
No right of appeal to the Hospital Managers.

Advocacy
No right to an independent mental health advocate (IMHA).

Mental Health Act Commission/Care Quality Commission
The right to be visited by and complain to the Mental Health Act Commission/ Care Quality Commission.

Duties on staff There is no rights leaflet for this section as it is used to return a person already subject to a section to the place they were detained. Those using Section

135(2) should inform the person of the power they are using to enter the premises, however the rights that apply are those of the section the person was under at the time they absconded from hospital.

Discharge	The section ends once the premises are entered and the person is removed. At this point, the person comes under the powers of the section they were subject to at the time they absconded.
Renewing the section	Section 135(2) cannot be renewed.
Forms	The magistrate will issue a Section 135(2) warrant.
Code of Practice	Informal attempts should be made to gain access first by asking the occupier of the premises for entry and only if this avenue has been unsuccessful, should forced entry under Section 135(2) be considered. Magistrates have to be satisfied that it is appropriate to issue a warrant. They are likely to ask applicants why they are applying for a warrant, whether reasonable attempts to enter without a warrant have been made and, if not, why not. When a warrant issued under Section 135(2) is being used, it is good practice for the police officer to be accompanied by a person with authority from the managers of the relevant hospital (or local social services authority).
Mental Health Act 2007	The 2007 Act made the following change to Section 135(2): ▪ The introduction of approved mental health professionals

Summary   The power for a police officer to take a person they have found in a public place, who appears in need of care or control, to a place of safety for assessment for up to 72 hours.

Legal criteria

A police officer finds, in a place to which the public have access, a person who appears to be suffering from mental disorder

and the person appears to be in immediate need of care or control

and the police officer considers it necessary in the interests of that person **or** for the protection of other persons, to remove them to a place of safety.

Powers

- *Detention* – the person can be detained for up to 72 hours in a place of safety (usually hospital or a police station). The person can be transferred to one or more other places of safety during the 72 hour period (for example from a police station to hospital) (see page 109).

- *Treatment* – the power to treat a person forcibly under the Act does not apply to this section. Treatment could only be given if the person has capacity and consents or, if they lack capacity to consent to treatment, by using the powers of the Mental Capacity Act 2005.

- *Absconding* – if the person absconds they can be forcibly returned to hospital by any authorised member of hospital staff or by the police.

Who is involved?   One *police officer*.

Time limits   The 72 hour period of detention begins when the person arrives at the place of safety.

Leave of absence   Does not apply as this is a short-term section for assessment.

Patient rights

Appeals
No right of appeal to the Mental Health Review Tribunal.
No right of appeal to the Hospital Managers.

Advocacy
No right to an independent mental health advocate (IMHA).

Mental Health Act Commission/Care Quality Commission
The right to be visited by and complain to the Mental Health Act Commission/ Care Quality Commission.

Duties on staff   Staff should take all practicable steps to ensure the patient understands their legal rights and provide this information both orally and in writing (the Department of Health produces standard rights leaflets).

Discharge	The section requires that the person is assessed by both a doctor (where possible Section 12 approved or approved clinician status) and an approved mental health professional within the 72 hours. If, following assessment, they do not believe a Section 2 or 3 to be appropriate, the Section 136 will end.
	The Code of Practice states that the person should not be held once a custody officer concludes that detention is no longer necessary.
Renewing the section	Section 136 cannot be renewed but a person can be detained further by the completion of a Section 2 or 3 before the Section 136 ends.
Forms	The police officer will complete a form for Section 136.
Code of Practice	*Place of safety*
	The preferred place of safety is hospital, however each area must decide on the most appropriate places of safety available to them and their use in different circumstances. A place of safety as defined in the Act is 'any police station, prison or remand centre, or any hospital the managers of which are willing temporarily to receive him'. For young people under 18 a place of safety has the same meaning as in the Children and Young Persons Act 1933 where a place of safety means a community home provided by a local authority or a controlled community home, police station, hospital, surgery, or any other suitable place, the occupier of which is willing temporarily to receive a child or young person.
	Police stations
	A police station should be used as a place of safety only in exceptional circumstances. A police station should not be assumed to be the automatic second choice if the first choice is not immediately available. Other available options, such as a residential care home or the home of a relative or friend of the person who is willing to accept them temporarily, should also be considered.
	Assessment by an approved mental health professional
	An approved mental health professional must always be called to assess a person under Section 136. However, if the doctor carries out the assessment before the approved mental health professional arrives and decides the person does not have a mental disorder under the Act, the person should be released from Section 136 immediately. The Code of Practice recommends that assessment should begin as soon as possible once the person arrives at the place of safety.
	Transfer
	A person may be transferred from one place of safety to another even if their assessment has already begun. If it cannot be avoided or would be in the person's best interests, another person may continue with their assessment at the second place of safety. Or, if they are not moved, another person may continue with their assessment even at the first place of safety.
	Except in emergencies, a doctor, an approved mental health professional or other appropriate healthcare professional able to assess the risk to the person's health or safety if they are transferred should be consulted.
	Because of the short-term nature of Section 136, it is crucial to note the time of arrival at the first place of safety and for this information to be passed on to any subsequent places of safety.

Case Law	Private land, even if adjacent to a public place, does not come within the meaning of a 'public place' under Section 136. In this case, a private garden with very little space between it and a public place could not be interpreted as a public place even if harm could be inflicted on passers-by from that garden.

(The case of: R v Leroy Lloyd Roberts [2003] EWCA Crim 2753, October 2003)

NOTE: The police have separate powers (not under the Mental Health Act) to enter private premises in any circumstances where they believe there is a 'breach of the peace'. |
| **Facts** | For the year ending March 2007, Section 136 was used 5,986 times in England. After assessment, 26% of people were placed on Section 2 or 3 and the remainder were either admitted informally or discharged[2]. |
| **Mental Health Act 2007** | The 2007 Act made the following changes to Section 136:
▪ The ability to move a person from one place of safety to another
▪ The introduction of approved mental health professionals |

If the powers of the Act are required to detain a person in hospital, the following sections may be used. They provide authority to detain a voluntary (informal) in-patient who refuses treatment and/or wishes to leave hospital or a person being cared for or treated under the Mental Capacity Act (because they lack capacity to consent) for whom detention under the Mental Health Act is now more appropriate perhaps due to restrictions upon the person's liberty becoming necessary.

Under the Act, a hospital is any NHS in-patient unit, either mental health or general. In addition, appropriately registered private hospitals and care homes are also considered to be hospitals in this context.

The hospital sections are:

Section	Professionals required	Duration
Section 2 *	Two doctors and an approved mental health professional or the nearest relative	up to 28 days
Section 3 *	Two doctors and an approved mental health professional or the nearest relative	up to 6 months and renewable
Section 5(2)	A doctor or an approved clinician	up to 72 hours
Section 5(4)	A nurse	up to 6 hours

Deprivation of Liberty Safeguards (see page 130)	*This new power is due to come into force in April 2009 as an amendment to the Mental Capacity Act. The power allows the detention of people who lack capacity.*	*up to 12 months and renewable*

* Sections 2 and 3 are the most commonly used detention powers of the Act and can be used both in hospital, to prevent a person leaving and in the community to bring a person into hospital and detain them there. Full details on Sections 2 and 3 are given in the previous chapter *Community to Hospital* (see pages 9 and 13).

Sections 5(2) and 5(4) are short-term emergency powers that are designed to prevent a voluntary in-patient discharging themselves. The duration of these sections allows time for the longer term powers of Section 2 or Section 3 to be applied.

It should be noted that the term *voluntary* or *informal* relates to a person with capacity to consent, freely giving their consent to the hospital admission or treatment. A patient lacking capacity to give such consent should not be admitted as a voluntary patient but can be admitted and treated under the powers of the Mental Capacity Act 2005 instead.

Note: The Act contains rules on conflicts of interest that those undertaking assessments to detain a person must follow (see page 127).

SECTION 5(2)
APPLICATION IN RESPECT OF A PATIENT ALREADY IN HOSPITAL

Summary
The power for a doctor or an approved clinician to detain a voluntary in-patient for up to 72 hours. It is designed to provide the time required to complete an application for Section 2 or 3 if the person wishes to leave hospital before the necessary arrangements for these applications can be made.

Legal criteria

The person is a voluntary in-patient in hospital

and it appears to the doctor (or approved clinician) in charge of the patient's treatment that an application ought to be made for a Section 2 or 3.

Powers
- *Detention* – the power to detain a person who is already in hospital for up to 72 hours.

- *Treatment* – the power to treat a person forcibly under the Act does not apply to this section. Treatment could only be given if the person has capacity and consents or, if they lack capacity to consent, by using the powers of the Mental Capacity Act.

- *Absconding* – if the person absconds they can be forcibly returned to hospital by any authorised member of hospital staff or by the police.

Who is involved?
A *doctor* or an *approved clinician (*who may not be a doctor*)* in charge of the patient's treatment or they can nominate another doctor or approved clinician, known as a deputy, of the same hospital. Hospitals should have a policy in place for such appointments. Only one doctor can be nominated. The nominated doctor cannot nominate a further doctor.

The doctor or approved clinician must give reasons why informal (voluntary) admission is no longer appropriate.

Time limits
The person can be detained for a maximum of 72 hours.

Leave of absence
Does not apply as this is a short-term section.

Patient rights

Appeals
No right of appeal to the Mental Health Review Tribunal.
No right of appeal to the Hospital Managers.

Advocacy
No right to an independent mental health advocate (IMHA).

Mental Health Act Commission/Care Quality Commission
The right to be visited by and complain to the Mental Health Act Commission/ Care Quality Commission.

Duties on staff
Staff should take all practicable steps to ensure the patient understands their legal rights and provide this information both orally and in writing (the Department of Health produces standard rights leaflets).

Working With The Mental Health Act

Discharge	There are a number of ways for the section to end:
	❖ It is decided that an assessment for further detention under Section 2 or 3 is not required.
	❖ The assessment for a Section 2 or 3 concludes that neither is required.
	❖ The section expires after the 72 hour period. Allowing the section to expire through passage of time would not be considered good practice as the assessment for Section 2 or 3 should take place within the 72 hour period.
Renewing the section	Section 5(2) cannot be renewed but a person can be detained further by the completion of a Section 2 or 3 before the Section 5(2) ends.
Forms	Form H1 – approved clinician's (or doctor's) report on hospital in-patient
Code of Practice	*Use of the Power* The Code warns against admitting people informally with the sole intention of then using the holding power. *Personal examination* Section 5(2) should only be used after the patient has been personally examined by the doctor or approved clinician. A doctor or approved clinician should not complete a Section 5(2) form and leave it on a ward (without the date or time on it) to be used in case the patient wishes to leave at some point in the future. *Nominated deputies* If nominated deputies are not approved clinicians (or doctors approved under Section 12 of the Act), they should wherever possible, seek advice from the person for whom they are deputising, or from someone else who is an approved clinician or Section 12 approved doctor, before using Section 5(2). *Out of hours* It is common practice, out of hours, for the junior on-call doctor at a hospital to be assigned the role of nominated deputy for the responsible clinicians at the site. In this role, they can use Section 5(2). *Transfer* Patients under Section 5(2) should not be transferred to another hospital. The Mental Health Act Commission/Care Quality Commission has produced a guidance note on transferring detained patients (see page 148).
Facts	Section 5(2) was used 8,039 times for the year ending March 2007, following which 35% of people were not placed on a further section[2].
Mental Health Act 2007	The 2007 Act made the following changes to Section 5(2): ▪ The introduction of approved clinicians who may use this power. ▪ Approved clinicians may not necessarily be doctors.

Summary The power for a nurse to detain a voluntary in-patient for up to six hours. The person has to indicate they wish to leave hospital and there has to be an immediate need to prevent this where a doctor or approved clinician is not available to complete a Section 5(2) instead. The section is intended as an emergency measure.

Legal criteria

A person is receiving treatment for *mental disorder* as an in-patient in hospital

and it appears to a nurse (of a prescribed level - see below) that the disorder is of such a degree that it is necessary for the person's health **or** safety **or** for the protection of others that they are immediately restrained from leaving hospital

and it is not practicable to secure the immediate attendance of a doctor or approved clinician to complete a Section 5(2) instead.

The words in italics are defined on page 154

Powers

• *Detention* – the power to detain a patient for up to six hours.

• *Treatment* – the power to treat a person forcibly under the Act does not apply to this section. Treatment could only be given if the person has capacity and consents or, if they lack capacity to consent, by using the powers of the Mental Capacity Act.

• *Absconding* – if the person absconds they can be forcibly returned to hospital by any authorised member of hospital staff or by the police.

Who is involved? *A nurse.* A registered nurse whose entry on the register of the Nursing & Midwifery Council indicates that the nurse's field of practice is either mental health or learning disabilities.

Time limits The section lasts for a maximum of six hours.

Leave of absence Does not apply as this is a short-term emergency section.

Patient rights

Appeals
No right of appeal to the Mental Health Review Tribunal.
No right of appeal to the Hospital Managers.

Advocacy
No right to an independent mental health advocate (IMHA).

Mental Health Act Commission/Care Quality Commission
The right to be visited by and complain to the Mental Health Act Commission/Care Quality Commission.

Duties on staff	Staff should take all practicable steps to ensure the patient understands their legal rights and provide this information both orally and in writing (the Department of Health produces standard rights leaflets).
Discharge	Section 5(4) is discharged when a doctor or approved clinician with authority to complete a Section 5(2) arrives and discharges the patient within the six hour period. It is not considered good practice for the section to run the full six hours and then expire without a doctor or approved clinician arriving.
Renewing the section	Section 5(4) cannot be renewed but when the doctor or approved clinician arrives a Section 5(2) can be applied instead. If this is the case, the six hour period of the Section 5(4) is included within the 72 hour period of the Section 5(2).
Forms	Form H2 – nurse's holding power
Code of Practice	The use of Section 5(4) is an emergency measure, and the doctor or approved clinician with the power to use Section 5(2) in respect of the patient should treat it as such and arrive as soon as possible. It is not possible for patients detained under Section 5(2) or 5(4) to be transferred to another hospital (because they are not detained by virtue of an application made under Part II of the Act). A nurse cannot be directed by others to use this power. Whether the legal criteria are met and the use of the power is appropriate is a matter for the professional judgment of the individual nurse concerned. The use of Section 5(4) should be closely monitored by hospital management.
Facts	Section 5(4) was used 1,406 times during the year ending March 2007 [2].
Mental Health Act 2007	The 2007 Act did not make any substantial changes to Section 5(4).

Community / Discharge options

Leave of Absence
Mental Health Act

Powers: person remains under the full powers of their detention section.

Leave can be ended at any time by the Responsible Clinician.

Any conditions can be attached to the leave.

Treatment can be given using the same powers that apply whilst a person is detained in hospital.

Limits: any leave over 7 consecutive days must show consideration of CTO as an alternative.

Can run for as long as the section does. Renewing a section whilst a person is on leave is possible but often the use of a CTO would be more appropriate.

Rights: appeal against the detaining section itself and right to independent mental health advocacy.

Responsibility: NHS controlled.

Community Treatment Order
Mental Health Act

Powers: mandatory conditions to see the Responsible Clinician and SOAD.

Secondary conditions that are flexible - such as where to live (but not enforceable).

The person may be recalled to hospital for up to 72 hours and given treatment (by force is necessary).

Treatment can only be given in the community if the person consents or they lack capacity to consent.

Limits: a person with capacity that refuses treatment can only be made to have it if they are recalled.

Can run for 6 months initially, and is renewable.

Rights: appeal against the order and right to independent mental health advocacy.

Responsibility: NHS controlled.

Guardianship
Mental Health Act

Powers: to take a person to a place to live and if they leave to return them.

A guardian supervises the case and makes decisions about where the person lives.

Guardians can be any person. Normally they are social workers.

Limits: the person cannot be detained in the place and they cannot be made to have treatment.

Can run for 6 months initially, and is renewable.

Rights: appeal against the order and right to independent mental health advocacy.

Responsibility: Local authority controlled.

Deprivation of Liberty
Mental Capacity Act

Powers: to detain a person for treatment or care (place them in an environment that deprives them of their liberty).

The power can be used in hospitals but in most cases will be used in care homes.

Limits: only for use in hospitals or care homes.

Only for use where the person lacks capacity to consent to care.

Can run for up to a year initially, and is renewable.

Rights: appeal against the order and right to independent mental capacity advocacy.

Responsibility: Local Authority or PCT controlled.

Discharge

Powers: None

If the person has capacity to refuse treatment or any health/social care service then this must be respected.

If the person lacks capacity to consent to treatment or other health or social care service the Mental Capacity Act can be used through an assessment of their 'best interests'.

The Mental Health Act provides two community powers: Guardianship (Section 7) which was part of the original 1983 Act and community treatment orders (Section 17A-G) inserted by the Mental Health Act 2007. The 2007 Act also repealed (removed) the old power of supervised discharge.

Note: Community treatment orders are also referred to as supervised community treatment in the Code of Practice. This guide uses the term community treatment orders.

Section	Name	Duration
Section 7	Guardianship	up to 6 months initially
Section 17A-G	Community treatment order	up to 6 months initially

Deprivation of Liberty Safeguards (see page 130)	*This new power is due to come into force in April 2009 as an amendment to the Mental Capacity Act.*	*up to 12 months initially*

Note: The Act contains rules on conflicts of interest that those undertaking assessments to detain a person must follow (see page 127).

Summary   A community based section that lasts for up to six months and may be renewed for further periods of time. It can be used both as an alternative to admitting people to hospital and as a route to discharging people from hospital.

Legal criteria

A person who is aged at least 16 years is suffering from *mental disorder*

and it is of a *nature or degree* to warrant the need for guardianship

and it is necessary in the interests of the welfare of the person **or** for the protection of others that guardianship is used.

The words in italics are defined on page 154

Powers
- *Residence* – the power to decide where the person lives and to take the person to their place of residence when the guardianship order is first made. If the person will not go voluntarily to the place or later absconds from that place, they are considered absent without leave and can be forcibly returned under Section 18(3) of the Act. However, this does not mean the person is detained there.

- *Appointments* – the power to require the person to attend appointments for treatment, occupation, education or training. This does not mean the person can be forced to attend appointments.

- *Access* – the power to require the person to see a doctor, approved mental health professional or other specified staff member at the person's place of residence. This does not mean the power to force entry to the person's residence to see them.

- *Treatment* – the person can only be given treatment with their consent. Or, if they lack capacity to consent, treatment can be given by using the powers of the Mental Capacity Act 2005.

Who is involved?   *Two doctors* – one of whom must be Section 12 approved (have experience of psychiatry) or have approved clinician status. If practicable, one doctor should already know the person
and
an *approved mental health professional* or the *nearest relative* (known as 'the applicant').

The applicant must state who the guardian will be, either a local authority (social services) or a named person. If the guardian is not a local authority, the proposed guardian must state in writing that they are willing to act as guardian and that the local authority have accepted this.

The application must also state the patient's age. If it is unknown, the applicant must state that the patient is believed to have attained the age of 16 (if that is indeed what they believe).

Working With The Mental Health Act

The approved mental health professional is required to consult the person's nearest relative (unless such consultation is not reasonably practicable or would involve unreasonable delay) as part of their assessment. If the relative objects to the section, it cannot proceed. A section can then only be completed if the relative is displaced by a court.

Time limits	There should be no more than five days between the medical examinations. The guardianship forms must be received by the local authority within 14 days of the second doctor's recommendation.

The applicant (approved mental health professional or nearest relative) must have seen the person in the last 14 days ending with the date they made their application. |
| **Leave of absence** | Does not apply as the person is living in the community. |
| **Patient rights** | Appeals
The right of appeal to the Mental Health Review Tribunal once during each period of detention.

The right of appeal to the local authority (social services).

Advocacy
The right to an independent mental health advocate (IMHA).

Mental Health Act Commission/Care Quality Commission
The right to be visited by and complain to the Mental Health Act Commission/ Care Quality Commission. |
| **Duties on staff** | Staff should take all practicable steps to ensure the patient understands their legal rights and provide this information both orally and in writing (the Department of Health produces standard rights leaflets).

The responsible local authority must arrange for a doctor (Section 12 approved or approved clinician status) to visit the person at least once a year. |
| **Discharge** | There are a number of ways for the section to end:

❖ Discharge by the responsible clinician authorised by the local social services authority

❖ Discharge by the responsible local authority (social services)

❖ Discharge by a Mental Health Review Tribunal

❖ Discharge by the nearest relative

❖ Lapse of the section at the end of the period of guardianship. Allowing the section to expire through passage of time would not be considered good practice as guardianship should end as soon as the legal criteria are no longer met.

❖ The use of Section 3 (if the person is admitted to hospital). However, where a person under guardianship is in hospital voluntarily or under Section 2, 4, 5(2) or 5(4), the guardianship order does not end but its powers are suspended until the person is discharged into the community (unless the guardianship order has expired in the meantime).

❖ Transfer to hospital under Section 19 of the Act. The transfer requires two medical recommendations plus social services approval (Form G8) and acts in such a way that on admission the guardianship is converted into a Section 3. |

Working With The Mental Health Act

Renewing the section	If a further period of guardianship is needed, the section may be renewed for another six months and thereafter, yearly. Consideration must be given to renewal two months before the current period of guardianship is due to expire (Form G9). Only the appropriate practitioner (the responsible clinician or, where the guardian is not the local authority, the nominated medical attendant of the patient) can renew the order. They must examine the person and consult with at least one other person who has been professionally involved with the person's treatment. The completed form has to be presented to the guardian and, if they are different, the local authority. The local authority must consider discharging the person when they receive the renewal form. Unless the guardian or local authority discharges the guardianship order, the renewal will take effect. *The legal criteria for renewal is:*

The person is suffering from mental disorder

⬇

and the disorder is of a nature or degree that warrants guardianship

⬇

and it is necessary in the interests of the person's welfare **or** for the protection of others that the person should remain under guardianship.

Forms	Form G1 - application by nearest relative **or** Form G2 - application by an approved mental health professional Form G3 or G4 - joint or single medical recommendations Form G5 - record of acceptance of guardianship application
Code of Practice	If a person consistently refuses the guardian's authority to make decisions, consideration should be given to an alternative guardian. A person subject to guardianship can be admitted to hospital informally for their mental health in the same way as other patients. Detention does not automatically become necessary just because they have been subject to guardianship. For those lacking capacity to make decisions for themselves about their health and social care, depending on the circumstances, the Mental Capacity Act 2005 may provide an alternative to the use of guardianship (see page 130). If a person has an attorney or deputy under the Mental Capacity Act, they do not have the authority to override any decisions which are the responsibility of the guardian.
Practical advice	*Admission to hospital (Section 116)* If the person is admitted to hospital there is a legal obligation on the guardian, if they are a local authority, to arrange regular visits to see the person. *Change of guardian (Section 10 (1)(2))* If the guardian dies or writes to the local authority to say they no longer wish to act as guardian, the power transfers to the local authority. In addition, if the guardian becomes incapacitated for any reason their functions may, during the period of incapacity, be performed by the local authority or someone approved by the local authority (Form G7 – transfer from one guardian to another).

Guardian not appropriate (Section 10(3))
If the guardian is not performing their functions properly, an approved mental health professional can apply to the County Court to have the guardian removed. The court would only remove the guardian if a judge thought the guardian was acting negligently or contrary to the welfare of the patient.

People involved in court proceedings (Section 22)
There are special provisions in the Act for people subject to guardianship who are also detained in custody by the courts.

Facts	During the year ending March 2007, there were 427 new guardianship orders made and by the end of March 2007 there were, in total, 926 people across England subject to a guardianship order[3].
Mental Health Act 2007	The 2007 Act made a number of changes to guardianship: • The power to take the person to their place of residence once the guardianship order is made • The single definition of mental disorder • The introduction of approved mental health professionals • The introduction of approved and responsible clinicians • The right to an independent mental health advocate (IMHA)

Summary   A community based section that runs for up to six months and may be renewed for further periods of time. Community treatment orders are also known by the term supervised community treatment (SCT).

Community treatment orders are unusual compared to other parts of the Act for two reasons. Firstly, in order to use them the person must initially be detained under Section 3, 37, 47, 48 or 45A (but no longer with a limitation direction). Secondly, when the community treatment order is applied, the original detaining section (3, 37, 47 or 48) is not discharged but rather 'suspended' and can be re-triggered by revocation of the order (explained in full below).

A patient subject to a community treatment order is known as a 'community patient' within the Act.

Legal criteria

A person is detained under Section 3, 37, 47 or 48

and the patient is suffering from *mental disorder* of a *nature or degree* which makes it appropriate for them to receive medical treatment

and it is necessary for their health or safety or for the protection of other persons that they should receive such treatment

and subject to them being liable to be recalled such treatment can be provided without them continuing to be detained in a hospital

and it is necessary that the responsible clinician should be able to exercise the power to recall the person to hospital

and *appropriate medical treatment* is available for them.

The words in italics are defined on page 154

Powers   **Mandatory conditions** – A community treatment order must contain two mandatory (enforceable) conditions:

1. the patient make themselves available for examination by the responsible clinician when they are considering renewing the order **and**
2. the patient make themselves available for examination by a second opinion appointed doctor as required under the treatment rules of the Act (for a Part 4A certificate).

Failure to comply with the mandatory conditions can trigger a recall of the person to hospital.

Discretionary conditions – In addition to the mandatory conditions, the order can also specify any number of further conditions at the discretion of the responsible clinician and approved mental health professional. These can only be made if they agree they are necessary or appropriate for one or more of the following reasons:

- to ensure that the patient receives medical treatment
- to prevent a risk of harm to the patient's health or safety
- to protect other people

Failure to comply with these further conditions does not in itself mean the person will be recalled. However such a failure can be taken into account in considering whether the patient needs to be recalled for treatment in hospital perhaps because of non-compliance with medication in the community (see *Recall* on the following page).

The responsible clinician may change (vary) or suspend the discretionary conditions specified in a community treatment order by completing Form CTO2.

Treatment – a community treatment order does not have the power to force treatment on a person with capacity whilst in the community. For full details of the treatment rules relating to community treatment orders see page 85.

Recall – the order contains the power to recall a person to hospital for treatment if certain criteria are met. The person may be conveyed (by force if necessary) to hospital and treated (again with force if needed).

Who is involved?	The *responsible clinician* makes the order in writing **and** an *approved mental health professional* must state in writing that they agree the patient meets the criteria of a community treatment order and that it is appropriate to make such an order.
Time limits	A community treatment order can initially last for a maximum of six months. It may be renewed for a further period of six months and then yearly.
Leave of absence	Does not apply as the person is in the community.
Patient rights	Appeals The right of appeal to the Mental Health Review Tribunal, once during each period of the community treatment order. The right of appeal to the Hospital Managers at any time and without limit to the number of appeals, at the discretion of the Hospital Managers. Advocacy The right to an independent mental health advocate (IMHA). Mental Health Act Commission/Care Quality Commission The right to be visited by and complain to the Mental Health Act Commission/ Care Quality Commission.
Duties on staff	Staff should take all practicable steps to ensure the person understands their legal rights and provide this information both orally and in writing (the Department of Health produces standard rights leaflets). If the person does not appeal to the Mental Health Review Tribunal six months after the beginning of the community treatment order (including any time spent on Section 2 and Section 3 before this without making an appeal) the hospital must refer their case to the Tribunal for an appeal hearing.

If the person has not had a Tribunal hearing for three years, their case must be referred to the Tribunal. If the person is under 18, this period is reduced to only one year before their case must be referred to a Tribunal.

If the person is recalled and the order is then revoked, the hospital has a duty to make an immediate referral to the Tribunal.

People subject to community treatment orders are entitled to after-care services under Section 117.

Transfer	A recalled patient can be transferred to another hospital (Form CTO6). In addition, the responsibility for a community treatment order patient can be transferred to another NHS Trust or other body (Form CTO10).
Recall	The responsible clinician *may* recall a community patient to hospital if:

the patient requires medical treatment in hospital for mental disorder
and
there would be a risk of harm to the health or safety of the patient or to other persons if the patient were not recalled to hospital for that treatment to be given
or
The responsible clinician *may* also recall a community patient to hospital if the patient fails to comply with either of the two mandatory conditions.

Failure to comply with the discretionary conditions can lead to recall although it is not a legal requirement to recall a patient. The recall may be considered appropriate where the patient's failure to adhere to the discretionary conditions would result in the above criteria being met.

Community patients already in hospital

The fact that a person subject to a community treatment order is already in hospital as a voluntary/informal patient does not preclude them from being formally recalled if the relevant criteria applies to them. If recalled, they will no longer be in hospital on a voluntary basis.

Recall procedure

To recall the community patient, the responsible clinician must complete Form CTO3. It must then be handed to the person. If the person cannot be found it can be delivered to the last known address for them and once deemed served (the day after it is left at the address, not necessarily 24 hours later) the power to recall the patient can be used. If the recall notice is posted (the Code of Practice advises against this), first class post should be used, however it will not be deemed served until the second day after it was posted.

Once the person attends hospital or is brought to hospital, the 72 hour period of the recall power starts, this is recorded on Form CTO4. The hospital has no longer than this period of time to decide whether the person can be released or the community treatment order is revoked.

The person does not have to be recalled to the hospital in which they were detained immediately prior to the community treatment order. If they are recalled to a different hospital, a copy of the recall notice should be sent to the hospital receiving the patient.

Absent without leave

If the person goes absent without leave during the 72 hour period, the normal absent without leave rules apply to them (see page 94).

Recall Outcomes

Outcome 1: Recall & revoke

At any point during the 72 hour period, the responsible clinician with the agreement of an approved mental health professional may revoke the community treatment order (completing Form CTO5) if they are satisfied that the person meets the criteria for detention under Section 3 (or the section the patient was under before being placed on the order - see above).

The effect of revoking the community treatment order is to re-start the suspended powers of the section the person was subject to prior to being placed on the order. The section is then deemed to begin afresh from the date of the revocation. So, if a person was recalled on the 1st March the Section 3 they were subject to before going onto to the community treatment order, it will be re-started and will run for six months from that date.

Once a community treatment order is revoked, the hospital has a duty to automatically refer the patient to the Mental Health Review Tribunal. The patient also retains their normal rights of appeal attached to the section.

Patients have a right to see an independent mental health advocate (IMHA).

Outcome 2: Recall & release

The responsible clinician may at any time during the 72 hour period release the person from recall. The person can then remain voluntarily or leave hospital and again be subject to the community treatment order powers as before.

Alternatively, if after 72 hours the responsible clinician has not revoked the community treatment order, the power of recall lapses and the person is free to leave the hospital subject to the community treatment order once again.

Discharge

There are a number of ways for a community treatment order to end:

❖ Discharge by the responsible clinician

❖ The person is recalled to hospital and the order is revoked (the person is then placed under their original detention section – 3, 37, 47 or 48)

❖ Discharge by a Mental Health Review Tribunal

❖ Discharge by a Hospital Managers' hearing

❖ Discharge by the nearest relative

❖ Lapse of the order at the end of the detaining period. Allowing the section to expire through passage of time would not be considered good practice as any detention should end as soon as the legal criteria are no longer met.

Renewing the section

Within the last two months of the community treatment order, the responsible clinician must examine the patient in order to decide whether the criteria for renewing the order will apply.

The section can be renewed by the responsible clinician for a further six month period and thereafter yearly (Form CTO7). The responsible clinician must examine the person and confirm they meet the legal criteria for a community treatment order. They must consult one or more other professionals involved with the patient and an approved mental health professional must agree with the renewal for it to come into effect.

Forms

Form CTO1 – community treatment order

The form must state the date on which the community treatment order should begin. This may be later than the date the form is completed to allow for arrangements to be made for the patient in the community.

| **Practical advice** | **Supervised discharge transfers** |
| | A six month transfer period is provided to transfer people subject to supervised discharge prior to 3rd November 2008 to a community treatment order instead. |

From 3rd November 2008, no new supervised discharge orders can be made and existing ones cannot be renewed. After 3rd November and before the expiry date of the supervised discharge order or before the 3rd May 2009 (whichever is sooner) the consultant in charge of the order must examine the person and within 14 days complete one of the following: a guardianship order, a community treatment order, Section 2 or 3 or discharge the person.

For further information see: *The Mental Health Act 2007 (Commencement No. 6 and After-care under Supervision: Savings, Modifications and Transitional Provisions) Order 2008*. The Department of Health has also produced guidance on this issue. Email: mentalhealthact2007@dh.gsi.gov.uk

| **Code of Practice** | *Consideration of community treatment order* |

A patient with a history of non-compliance with treatment plans or medication whilst in the community, resulting in a relapse, may justify the use of a community treatment order as opposed to discharge.

Involvement of patients
Although patients do not have to consent to the community treatment order, their involvement and co-operation is needed in making the order. For example, how and where the treatment will be given whilst they are in the community. The discretionary conditions should be made with the Code of Practice's principles in mind and explained to the patient (see page 4).

The conditions
The conditions should be kept to a minimum number consistent with achieving their purpose. They should restrict the patient's liberty as little as possible while still achieving their purpose. The conditions should have a clear rationale and be clearly and precisely expressed, so that the patient can readily understand what is expected.

Although the responsible clinician can vary the discretionary conditions without agreement from the approved mental health professional, it would not be considered good practice to do so where a community treatment order had been made recently.

Recall
The responsible clinician must be satisfied that the recall criteria are met before using this power. Any action should be proportionate to the level of risk. For some patients, the risk arising from a failure to comply with treatment could indicate an immediate need for recall. In other cases, negotiation with the patient, the nearest relative and any carer (unless the patient objects or it is not reasonably practicable to consult with them) may resolve the problem and so avert the need for recall.

Recall to hospital for treatment should not become a regular event for any patient. If recall is being used frequently, the responsible clinician should review the patient's treatment plan to consider whether it could be made more acceptable to the patient, or whether, in the individual circumstances of the case, the community treatment order is no longer appropriate.

| **Mental Health Act 2007** | The 2007 Act removed the previous community power known as supervised discharge and replaced it with community treatment orders. |

FORENSIC (COURT AND PRISON) SECTIONS

Sections that relate to court and criminal proceedings are contained in Part III of the Act. Part III is one of the most complex areas of the legislation due to the number of sections and the individual rules that apply to each one. The different detention sections relate to the various stages in the criminal justice process (see the diagram below). In addition, because of the nature of some offences, restrictions are applied which lead to the involvement of the Ministry of Justice (see *Forensic Restricted Sections*, page 64).

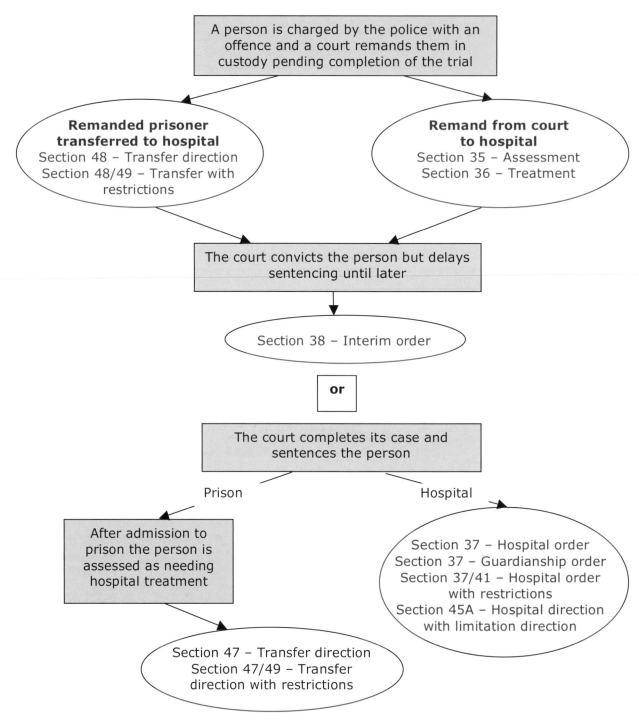

Summary A person accused of a crime may be sent by a court to hospital for assessment of their mental health for a period of up to 28 days. The section is renewable for further periods of 28 days, up to a maximum of 12 weeks. The purpose of the section is for the hospital to provide the court with a report on the person's mental disorder.

Legal criteria

Crown Court: the person is awaiting trial for an offence punishable by imprisonment, or has been arraigned (accused) for such an offence but has not yet been sentenced or otherwise dealt with for the offence

or

Magistrates' Court: the person has been convicted of an offence punishable on summary conviction with imprisonment, or is charged with an offence punishable with imprisonment and either the court is satisfied that they did the act or made the omission charged or that the person has consented to the use of Section 35

and the court is satisfied on the written or oral evidence of a doctor that there is reason to suspect the person is suffering from *mental disorder*

and it would be impracticable for a report on their mental condition to be completed if they were remanded on bail.

The words in italics are defined on page 154

Powers
- *Detention* – the power to detain the person for up to 28 days initially.

- *Treatment* – treatment can only be given if the person has capacity and consents or, if they lack capacity to consent to treatment, by using the powers of the Mental Capacity Act 2005.

- *Absconding* – if the person absconds they can be arrested (without a warrant) by a police officer and taken to court. The court may choose to end the section and continue with the original criminal proceedings.

Who is involved? A *Magistrates' Court* or *Crown Court* makes the order
and
a *doctor* who is Section 12 approved (has experience of psychiatry) or has approved clinician status gives written or oral evidence to the court.

Time limits For the Section 35 order to be valid, the court must be satisfied that the person will be admitted to hospital within seven days of the order being made. Evidence of this must be given to the court by the doctor who produces the report or by a person representing the managers of that hospital. The hospital must then admit and detain the person.

Leave of absence The Department of Health's Reference Guide to the Act[4] states: '*Patients remanded to hospital under Section 35 or 36 may not be given leave of absence from the hospital without the express agreement of the remanding court. Nor may the hospital managers transfer them to another hospital. If necessary, an application may be made to the court for a new remand order.*'

Patient rights	Appeals To obtain, at their own expense, a report by another approved clinician or psychiatrist and use this to apply to the court for the section to be discharged. No right of appeal to the Mental Health Review Tribunal or Hospital Managers. Advocacy The right to an independent mental health advocate (IMHA). Mental Health Act Commission/Care Quality Commission The right to be visited by and complain to the Mental Health Act Commission/ Care Quality Commission.
Duties on staff	Staff should take all practicable steps to ensure the patient understands their legal rights and provide this information both orally and in writing (the Department of Health produces standard rights leaflets).
Discharge	There are a number of ways for the section to end: ❖ The court may discharge the section at any time it appears appropriate to do so or when the court case is concluded and sentence passed. ❖ The court is presented with an independent medical report, initiated by the patient, which states they do not have a mental disorder. ❖ The hospital reports that the person does not need further assessment.
Renewing the section	If more time is needed to complete the assessment, the court can extend the section for further periods of 28 days, up to a maximum of 12 weeks. To renew the section, an approved clinician must give written or oral evidence to the court. If the person is legally represented, they do not have to attend the court hearing but their legal representative must. The court can also extend the person's detention at the end of the criminal process by sentencing them to hospital under Section 37.
Forms	The court issues a Section 35 remand order.
Code of Practice	The court directs responsibility for transporting the person to hospital after making the order. However, once admitted to hospital, the hospital is responsible for returning the person to court for future hearings and also for providing an escort for the person when travelling to court from hospital.
Practical advice	This section is not covered by the treatment powers of the Act so medication can only be given if the person consents. The Mental Capacity Act 2005 could be used if the person lacks capacity to consent. However, if the person has capacity and refuses treatment they can be referred back to court with a recommendation for either a Section 36 (but only a Crown Court can make this order) or a Section 37. If the court cannot provide a hearing for the above and treatment is assessed as being urgent, it is possible to complete a Section 2 or 3 whilst a person is also subject to Section 35 so that the person is effectively detained under two sections. This enables the person to be given treatment without their consent.
Facts	104 Section 35 orders were made during the year ending March 2007 [2].
Mental Health Act 2007	The 2007 Act made the following changes to Section 35: ▪ The single definition of mental disorder ▪ The introduction of approved and responsible clinicians ▪ The right to an independent mental health advocate (IMHA)

Summary   A person on remand is sent by the Crown Court to hospital for treatment lasting up to 28 days. The section can be extended for up to 12 weeks in total.

Legal criteria

Crown Court: A person charged with an offence punishable with imprisonment (except offences with a fixed sentence – i.e. murder) is either in custody awaiting trial or awaiting sentence following trial

and they are suffering from *mental disorder* of a *nature or degree* which makes it appropriate for them to be detained in hospital for medical treatment

and *appropriate medical treatment* is available for them.

The words in italics are defined on page 154

Powers

- *Detention* – the power to detain the person for up to 28 days initially.

- *Treatment* – the person can be given treatment for mental disorder with or without their consent under Part 4 of the Act (see page 79).

- *Absconding* – if the person absconds they can be arrested (without a warrant) by a police officer and taken to court. The court may choose to end the section and continue with the original criminal proceedings.

Who is involved?   *Two doctors,* one of whom must be Section 12 approved (have experience of psychiatry) or have approved clinician status. The doctors can submit written reports to the court or attend in person to give an oral report. Both doctors can be from the same NHS Trust
and
a *Crown Court* (a Magistrates' Court cannot make this order).

Time limits   The person must be admitted to hospital within seven days of the order being made.

Leave of absence   The Department of Health's Reference Guide to the Act[4] states: *'Patients remanded to hospital under section 35 or 36 may not be given leave of absence from the hospital without the express agreement of the remanding court. Nor may the hospital managers transfer them to another hospital. If necessary, an application may be made to the court for a new remand order'.*

Patient rights   Appeals
The right to obtain, at their own expense, a report by another approved clinician or psychiatrist and use this to apply to the court for the section to be discharged.

No right of appeal to the Mental Health Review Tribunal.

No right of appeal to the Hospital Managers.

<u>Advocacy</u>
The right to an independent mental health advocate (IMHA).

<u>Mental Health Act Commission/Care Quality Commission</u>
The right to be visited by and complain to the Mental Health Act Commission/ Care Quality Commission.

Duties on staff	Staff should take all practicable steps to ensure the patient understands their legal rights and provide this information both orally and in writing (the Department of Health produces standard rights leaflets).
Discharge	There are a number of ways for the section to end: ❖ The court may discharge the section at any time it appears appropriate to do so or when the court case is concluded and sentence passed. ❖ The court is presented with an independent medical report, initiated by the patient, stating they do not have a mental disorder. ❖ The hospital reports that the person does not need treatment.
Renewing the section	The section can be renewed for further periods of 28 days up to a total of 12 weeks. To do this, the responsible clinician provides a written report to the court, or attends in person and requests a further period of time. The court will decide whether to extend the section or not. If the person is legally represented they do not have to attend the hearing but their legal representative must. The court can continue hospital detention at the end of the criminal justice process by sentencing the person to hospital under Section 37.
Forms	The Crown Court issues a Section 36 remand order.
Code of Practice	The court directs responsibility for organising the transportation of the person to hospital after making the order. However, once admitted to hospital, the hospital is responsible for returning the person to court for future hearings and also for providing an escort for the person when travelling to court from hospital. Once the person is at court, they come under the supervision of the police or prison officers there.
Facts	Section 36 is rarely used and for the year ending March 2007, there were only 16 recorded cases[2].
Mental Health Act 2007	The 2007 Act made a number of changes to Section 36: ▪ The single definition of mental disorder ▪ The introduction of approved and responsible clinicians ▪ The additional detention criteria of appropriate medical treatment being available ▪ The changes to the treatment rules of the Act ▪ The right to an independent mental health advocate (IMHA)

Summary   A court sentences a person to hospital for treatment (or to guardianship, see page 52) for up to six months. The section can be renewed for further periods of time. Section 37 operates like a Section 3 once the person is admitted to hospital. A Section 37 may also be made with a restriction order from the Ministry of Justice attached. It is then known as Section 37/41 (see page 65).

Legal criteria

Magistrates' Court: a person is convicted of an offence punishable on summary conviction with imprisonment **or** charged with such an offence and the court is satisfied the person has committed the act or offence they are charged with

or

Crown Court: a person is convicted of an offence punishable with imprisonment

and the person is suffering from *mental disorder*

and the mental disorder is of a *nature or degree* which makes it appropriate for them to be detained in hospital for treatment

and *appropriate medical treatment* is available

and the court is of the opinion that the most suitable method of dealing with the person is by means of this section.

The words in italics are defined on page 154

Powers   • *Detention* – the power to detain the person for up to six months initially.

• *Treatment* – the person can be given treatment for mental disorder with or without their consent (see page 79).

• *Absconding* – if the person absconds, they can be forcibly returned to hospital by any authorised member of hospital staff or by the police.

Who is involved?   *Two doctors,* one of whom must be Section 12 approved (have experience of psychiatry) or have approved clinician status. The doctors can provide written recommendations or give oral evidence before the court. The doctors can work for the same NHS Trust
and
a *Crown Court or Magistrates' Court* which makes the order.

Time limits   The person must be admitted to hospital within 28 days of the order being made. If they are not admitted immediately, they can be detained for up to 28 days in a place of safety whilst a hospital bed is arranged.

Leave of absence   The responsible clinician can grant leave of absence for any period of time. For the responsible clinician to grant any period of leave over seven consecutive days, they must first consider whether the patient could be placed on a community treatment order instead.

Patient rights	Appeals The right to appeal to the Crown Court or Court of Appeal to have the conviction quashed or a different sentence imposed. The right of appeal to the Mental Health Review Tribunal, but only in the second six months and then once in each subsequent period of detention. The patient's nearest relative has the same right. The right of appeal to the Hospital Managers at any time and without limit to the number of appeals, at the discretion of the Hospital Managers. Advocacy The right to an independent mental health advocate (IMHA). Mental Health Act Commission/Care Quality Commission The right to be visited by and complain to the Mental Health Act Commission/ Care Quality Commission.
Duties on staff	Staff should take all practicable steps to ensure the patient understands their legal rights and provide this information both orally and in writing (the Department of Health produces standard rights leaflets). If the patient has not had a Mental Health Review Tribunal hearing for three years from the date of the hospital order (or one year if under 18), the hospital must refer their case to the Tribunal. The provision of after-care services under Section 117 upon discharge. Schedule 6 (victim's rights) of the Mental Health Act 2007 introduced a number of duties on hospitals detaining people under Section 37 where the offence committed by the patient was of a sexual or violent nature. The victims of such offences have the right to be informed by the hospital when certain decisions are being made in relation to the Section 37. For full details see Sections 36A to 44B of the Mental Health Act 1983 and Schedule 6 (as amended by the 2007 Act).
Discharge	There are a number of ways for the section to end: ❖ Discharge by the responsible clinician ❖ Discharge by a Mental Health Review Tribunal ❖ Discharge by a Hospital Managers' hearing ❖ Discharge by the Crown Court or Court of Appeal (this may result in the person being sentenced again but under criminal law) ❖ Transfer (discharge) to a community treatment order or guardianship ❖ Lapse of the section at the end of the detaining period. Allowing the section to expire through passage of time would not be considered good practice as any detention should end as soon as the legal criteria are no longer met.
Renewing the section	The section can be renewed before it ends by the responsible clinician for a further six month period and thereafter yearly. The renewal criteria and process are the same as for Section 3 (see page 13).
Forms	The court issues a Section 37 hospital order.
Code of Practice	If, at the time of sentencing, doctors are not satisfied that a hospital order is appropriate, they should consider recommending a Section 38 interim order (see pages 55).

Working With The Mental Health Act

The court will direct who is responsible for transporting the person to hospital after the order is made.

Practical advice	With Section 37, the court passes responsibility for the person over to the hospital. Once in hospital, the court has no further input and theoretically the responsible clinician could discharge the section immediately. A person's mental state at the time of the offence is not part of the consideration for applying Section 37.
Facts	Section 37 is the most used non-restricted forensic section. For the year ending March 2007, there were 248 admissions to hospital from Section 37 court orders[2].
Mental Health Act 2007	The 2007 Act made a number of changes to Section 37: • The single definition of mental disorder • The introduction of approved and responsible clinicians • The additional detention criteria of appropriate medical treatment being available • A second professional must agree before the section can be renewed • The ability to discharge via a community treatment order • Changes to the treatment rules under the Act • The right to an independent mental health advocate (IMHA) • Changes to the automatic referral periods for Tribunal hearings • Giving consideration to the use of a community treatment order before any leave of absence over seven consecutive days is granted • Rights for victims of sexual or violent offences

SECTION 37
GUARDIANSHIP ORDER

Summary A court sentences a person to guardianship in the community for up to six months, which may be extended for further periods of time. It operates like a Section 7 guardianship order.

Legal criteria

> ***Magistrates' Court:*** a person is convicted of an offence punishable on summary conviction with imprisonment **or** charged with such an offence and the court is satisfied the person has committed the act or offence they are charged with
>
> **or**
>
> ***Crown Court:*** a person is convicted of an offence punishable with imprisonment
>
>
>
> **and** the person is suffering from a *mental disorder*
>
>
>
> **and** the person has reached the age of 16 and the mental disorder is of a *nature or degree* which warrants their reception into guardianship
>
>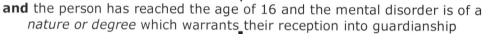
>
> **and** the court is of the opinion that the most suitable method of dealing with the case is by means of this section.
>
> *The words in italics are defined on page 154*

Powers

- *Residence* – the power to decide where the person lives and to take the person by force to their place of residence when the guardianship order is first made. If the person absconds from this place, they can be forcibly returned. However, this does not mean the person can be detained there.

- *Appointments* – the power to require the person to attend appointments for treatment, occupation, education or training. However, this does not mean the person can be forced to attend appointments.

- *Access* – the power to require the person to see any doctor, approved mental health professional or other member of staff at the person's place of residence. However, this does not mean the power to force entry to the person's residence.

- *Treatment* – the person can only be given treatment with their consent. If they lack capacity to consent, the powers of the Mental Capacity Act 2005 may be used to provide the treatment instead.

Who is involved? *Two doctors,* one of whom must be Section 12 approved (have experience of psychiatry) or have approved clinician status. The doctors can provide written recommendations or give oral evidence before the court. The doctors can work for the same NHS Trust
and
a *Crown Court or Magistrates' Court* which makes the order.

The court will name a local authority (social services) or a person approved by the local authority to act as guardian.

Time limits	No time limits apply except for the length of the Section 37 guardianship order itself.
Leave of absence	Does not apply as the person is in the community.
Patient rights	<u>Appeals</u> The right of appeal to the Crown Court or Court of Appeal to have the conviction quashed or a different sentence imposed. The right of appeal to the Mental Health Review Tribunal once during each period of guardianship. The right of appeal to the local authority (social services). <u>Advocacy</u> The right to an independent mental health advocate (IMHA). <u>Mental Health Act Commission/Care Quality Commission</u> The right to be visited by and complain to the Mental Health Act Commission/ Care Quality Commission.
Duties on staff	Staff should take all practicable steps to ensure the patient understands their legal rights and provide this information both orally and in writing (the Department of Health produces standard rights leaflets). If the person has not had a Mental Health Review Tribunal hearing for three years (or one year for a person under 18), the local authority must refer their case to the Tribunal. Schedule 6 (victim's rights) of the Mental Health Act 2007 introduced a number of duties on hospitals detaining people under Section 37 where the offence committed by the patient was of a sexual or violent nature. The victims of such offences have the right to be informed by the hospital when certain decisions are being made in relation to the Section 37. For full details see Sections 36A to 44B of the Mental Health Act and Schedule 6 (as amended by the 2007 Act).
Discharge	There are a number of ways for the section to end: ❖ Discharge by the responsible clinician ❖ Discharge by a Mental Health Review Tribunal ❖ Discharge by the local authority ❖ Discharge by the Crown Court or Court of Appeal (this may result in the person being sentenced again but under criminal law) ❖ Lapse of the section at the end of the period of guardianship. Allowing the section to expire through passage of time would not be considered good practice because the guardianship should end as soon as the legal criteria are no longer met.
Renewing the section	The section can be renewed before it ends by the responsible clinician for a further six month period and thereafter yearly.
Forms	The court issues a Section 37 guardianship order.

Practical advice	With Section 37, the court places the person into guardianship. Once under guardianship, the court has no further input or responsibility.
Mental Health Act 2007	The 2007 Act made a number of changes to Section 37 guardianship: • The single definition of mental disorder • The introduction of responsible clinicians and approved clinicians • A second professional must agree to the section being renewed • Changes to the treatment rules under the Act • The right to an independent mental health advocate (IMHA) • Changes to the automatic referral periods for Tribunal hearings • Rights for victims of sexual and violent offences

```
┌─────────────────────────────────────────────┐
│               SECTION 38                      │
│          INTERIM HOSPITAL ORDER               │
└─────────────────────────────────────────────┘
```

Summary   A court order that allows a hospital to detain a convicted offender, initially for up to 12 weeks, in order to assess whether a full hospital order (Section 37) is appropriate. The section can be extended for up to a maximum of one year.

Legal criteria

A person convicted by a Crown Court or Magistrates' Court
of an offence punishable with imprisonment

↓

and the person is suffering from *mental disorder*

↓

and there is reason to suppose that the mental disorder from which the person is suffering is such that it may be appropriate for a hospital order (Section 37) to be made.

The words in italics are defined on page 154

Powers
- *Detention* – the power to detain the person for up to 12 weeks initially.

- *Treatment* – the person can be given treatment for mental disorder with or without their consent (see page 79).

- *Absconding* – if the person absconds they can be arrested (without a warrant) by a police officer and then taken to court. The court may choose to end the section and deal with the person in another way.

Who is involved?   *Two doctors,* one of whom must be Section 12 approved (have experience of psychiatry) or have approved clinician status. One doctor must be from the NHS Trust that will treat the person and both doctors may work for the same NHS Trust. The doctors can provide written medical recommendations or give oral evidence before the court
and
a *Crown Court or Magistrates' Court* which makes the order.

Time limits   The person must be admitted to hospital within 28 days of the order being made.

Leave of absence   Patients under Section 38 cannot be given leave.

Patient rights   Appeals
The right of appeal to the Crown Court or Court of Appeal to have the conviction quashed or a different sentence imposed.

No right of appeal to the Mental Health Review Tribunal.

No right of appeal to the Hospital Managers.

Advocacy
The right to an independent mental health advocate (IMHA).

Mental Health Act Commission/Care Quality Commission

The right to be visited by and complain to the Mental Health Act Commission/ Care Quality Commission.

Duties on staff	Staff should take all practicable steps to ensure the patient understands their legal rights and provide this information both orally and in writing (the Department of Health produces standard rights leaflets).
Discharge	There are a number of ways for the section to end: ❖ Discharge by the Crown Court or Court of Appeal (this may result in the person being sentenced again but under criminal law). ❖ Following the hospital's assessment, the court may decide to make a Section 37 hospital order (thereby ending the court's involvement) or deal with the person in some other way.
Renewing the section	The section initially lasts for up to 12 weeks and can then be renewed by the court for further periods of up to 28 days. However, the order cannot be renewed for a total of more than twelve months. Extensions are made on the written or oral evidence of the responsible clinician to the court. If the person is legally represented, they do not have to attend the court hearing but their legal representative must.
Forms	The Crown Court or Magistrates' Court issues a Section 38 order.
Code of Practice	The court will direct who is responsible for transporting the person to hospital after the order is made. However, once admitted to hospital, the hospital is responsible for returning the person to court for future hearings and for providing an escort for the person when travelling from hospital to court. The police may be asked to assist with this if necessary. Once the person is at court, they come under the supervision of the police or prison officers there. However, the Code advises that having regard to the person's needs, the hospital staff should also stay with them.
Mental Health Act 2007	The 2007 Act made the following changes to Section 38: ▪ The single definition of mental disorder ▪ The introduction of approved clinicians and responsible clinicians ▪ Changes to the treatment rules under the Act ▪ The right to an independent mental health advocate (IMHA)

Summary The transfer of a sentenced prisoner to hospital and their detention there for up to six months initially. Once in hospital, the section operates like a Section 37 hospital order. A Section 47 is usually made with a restriction order from the Ministry of Justice attached. It is then known as Section 47/49 (see page 71).

Legal criteria

The person is serving a sentence of imprisonment

↓

and the Secretary of State is satisfied they are suffering from *mental disorder*

↓

and the mental disorder is of a *nature or degree* which makes it appropriate for them to be detained in hospital for treatment

↓

and *appropriate medical treatment is available* for them

↓

and the Secretary of State, having regard to the public interest and all the circumstances, may direct that the person is removed to and detained in hospital.

The words in italics are defined on page 154

Powers
- *Detention* – the power to detain the person for up to six months initially.

- *Treatment* – the person can be given treatment for mental disorder with or without their consent (see page 79).

- *Absconding* – if the person absconds they can be forcibly returned to hospital by any authorised member of hospital staff or by the police.

Who is involved? *Two doctors,* one of whom must be Section 12 approved (have experience of psychiatry) or have approved clinician status. One of the doctors should work at the NHS Trust which is to receive the person. Both doctors can work for the same NHS Trust
and
the *Ministry of Justice* which agrees and issues the transfer direction.

The Ministry of Justice is not obliged to agree to a Section 47 despite two medical recommendations being made. It will consider whether the prisoner can be safely contained by the hospital taking into account a number of risk factors including the nature of the offence, the length of the sentence and the risk of absconding.

Time limits The person must be admitted to hospital within 14 days of the Section 47 order being made (starting with the day it was given). If this does not happen, a new transfer direction would be needed.

Leave of absence The responsible clinician can grant leave (Section 17) for any period of time. For the responsible clinician to grant any period of leave over seven consecutive days, they must first consider whether the patient could be placed on a community treatment order instead.

Patient rights	Appeals The right of appeal to the Mental Health Review Tribunal in the first six months and then once in each subsequent period of detention. The right of appeal to the Hospital Managers at any time and without limit to the number of appeals, at the discretion of the Hospital Managers. Advocacy The right to an independent mental health advocate (IMHA). Mental Health Act Commission/Care Quality Commission The right to be visited by and complain to the Mental Health Act Commission/ Care Quality Commission.
Duties on staff	Staff should take all practicable steps to ensure the patient understands their legal rights and provide this information both orally and in writing (the Department of Health produces standard rights leaflets). If the person has not had a Mental Health Review Tribunal hearing for three years (or one year for those under 18), the hospital must refer their case to the Tribunal. The provision of after-care services under Section 117 upon discharge. Schedule 6 (victim's rights) of the Mental Health Act 2007 introduced a number of duties on hospitals detaining people under Section 47 where the offence committed by the patient was of a sexual or violent nature. The victims of such offences have the right to be informed by the hospital when certain decisions are being made in relation to the Section 47. For full details see Sections 36A to 44B of the Mental Health Act 1983 and Schedule 6 (as amended by the 2007 Act).
Discharge	There are a number of ways for the section to end: ❖ Discharge by the responsible clinician ❖ Discharge by a Mental Health Review Tribunal ❖ Discharge by a Hospital Managers' hearing ❖ Discharge subject to a community treatment order
Renewing the section	The section can be renewed before it ends by the responsible clinician for a further six month period and yearly thereafter.
Forms	The Ministry of Justice issues a Section 47 transfer direction.
Code of Practice	A prisoner's need for in-patient treatment should be acted upon quickly. The responsible NHS Commissioners should ensure that the transfer of prisoners with mental disorders is carried out at the same speed as those admitted from the community for treatment or care. If unacceptable delays occur after it is decided that a patient needs treatment, these should be actively monitored and investigated. The person should not be transferred back to prison unless the prison and hospital jointly meet to discuss their after-care (Section 117).

Practical advice	A Section 47 without a restriction order operates like a Section 37 (hospital order) when the person is admitted to hospital. The Ministry produces a guide to the use of this power – please see the beginning of the chapter on *Forensic Restricted Sections* for full details (page 64).
Facts	For the year ending March 2007, Section 47 was only used 40 times[2].
Mental Health Act 2007	The 2007 Act made a number of changes to Section 47: • The single definition of mental disorder • The introduction of responsible clinicians and approved clinicians • The additional detention criteria of appropriate medical treatment being available • The right to an independent mental health advocate (IMHA) • The requirement to consider a community treatment order before a period of leave over seven consecutive days is granted • The ability to discharge the patient subject to a community treatment order • A second professional to agree to renewal before it can go ahead • Changes to the automatic referral periods for Tribunal hearings • Rights for victims of sexual or violent offences

SECTION 48
REMOVAL TO HOSPITAL OF UNSENTENCED PRISONERS

Summary The transfer of an unsentenced prisoner to hospital and their detention there. In the majority of cases a Section 48 is made with a restriction order from the Ministry of Justice attached. It is then known as Section 48/49 (see page 75).

Legal criteria

A civil prisoner committed to prison by a court for a limited term, or detained under the Immigration Act 1971 or Section 62 of the Nationality, Immigration and Asylum Act 2002

and the Secretary of State is satisfied that the person is suffering from *mental disorder* of a *nature or degree* which makes it appropriate for them to be detained and treated in hospital

and *appropriate medical treatment is available*

and the person is in urgent need of such treatment.

The words in italics are defined on page 154

Powers
- *Detention* – the power to detain the person until the court process is concluded.

- *Treatment* – the person can be given treatment for mental disorder with or without their consent (see page 79).

- *Absconding* – if the person absconds they can be forcibly returned to hospital by any authorised member of hospital staff or by the police.

Who is involved?
Two doctors, one of whom must be Section 12 approved (have experience of psychiatry) or have approved clinician status. Both doctors may be from the same NHS Trust
and
the *Ministry of Justice* which agrees and issues the transfer direction.

It is important to note that the Ministry of Justice is not obliged to agree to a Section 48 despite two medical recommendations being made. It will consider whether the prisoner can be safely contained by the hospital taking into account a number of risk factors including the nature of the offence, their behaviour in prison and the risk of absconding.

Time limits
The person must be admitted to hospital within 14 days of the Section 48 being made by the Secretary of State.

Leave of absence
The responsible clinician can grant leave of absence (Section 17) for any period of time. For the responsible clinician to grant any period of leave over seven consecutive days, they must first consider whether the patient could be placed on a community treatment order instead.

Patient rights	Appeals
	The right of appeal to the Mental Health Review Tribunal once in the first six months and then once in each subsequent period of detention.
	The right of appeal to the Hospital Managers at any time and without limit to the number of appeals, at the discretion of the Hospital Managers.
	Advocacy
	The right to an independent mental health advocate (IMHA).
	Mental Health Act Commission/Care Quality Commission
	The right to be visited by and complain to the Mental Health Act Commission/ Care Quality Commission.
Duties on staff	Staff should take all practicable steps to ensure the patient understands their legal rights and provide this information both orally and in writing (there is a standard Department of Health rights leaflet).
	If the person has not had a Mental Health Review Tribunal hearing for three years (or one year for those under 18), the hospital must refer their case to the Tribunal.
	The provision of after-care services under Section 117 upon discharge.
	Schedule 6 (victim's rights) of the Mental Health Act 2007 introduced a number of duties on hospitals detaining patients under Section 48 where the offence committed by the patient was of a sexual or violent nature. The victims of such offences have the right to be informed by the hospital when certain decisions are being made in relation to the Section 48. For full details see Sections 36A to 44B of the Mental Health Act and Schedule 6 (as amended by the 2007 Act).
Discharge	There are a number of ways for the section to end:
	❖ The responsible clinician may inform the Ministry of Justice or court that the person no longer requires treatment in hospital or that no effective treatment can be provided for them
	❖ Discharge by a Mental Health Review Tribunal
	❖ Discharge by a Hospital Managers' hearing
	❖ Transfer (discharge) to a community treatment order
	In all of the above cases, the Ministry of Justice and court must be informed as they may issue an order for the person to be returned to prison or for immigration detainees, returned to detention.
	❖ The legal proceedings to which the person is subject ends and they are sentenced.
Renewing the section	Section 48 remains in place until the court or Ministry of Justice direct that it should end.
Forms	The Ministry of Justice issues a Section 48 transfer direction.
Practical Advice	The Ministry of Justice produces a guide to the use of this power – see page 64 for details.

Facts	There were just 11 people transferred under Section 48 orders for the year ending March 2007. This compares with 473 people transferred via Section 48/49 during the same period[2].
Mental Health Act 2007	The 2007 Act made a number of changes to Section 48: • The single definition of mental disorder • The introduction of approved clinicians and responsible clinicians • The additional detention criteria of appropriate medical treatment being available • The ability to discharge the patient subject to a community treatment order • Changes to the treatment rules under the Act • The right to an independent mental health advocate (IMHA) • Changes to the automatic referral periods for Tribunal hearings • Rights for victims of violent or sexual offences

Restricted sections are applied when it is thought that a person requires extra supervision for the protection of the public. The order is either made at the point of sentencing by a court or through the transfer of a prisoner to hospital by the Secretary of State for the Ministry of Justice. The restriction means that decisions concerning leave, transfer and discharge must involve the Ministry of Justice. Under the Act, restricted sections are the responsibility of the Secretary of State, however in practice a department of the Ministry of Justice undertakes the legal requirements on behalf of the Minister.

Contact

Mental Health Unit
The Ministry of Justice, 2nd Floor, Fry Building, 2 Marsham Street, London SW1P 4DF

Tel: 020 7035 1484   Fax: 020 7035 8974   Website: www.noms.justice.gov.uk

Guidance

The Mental Health Unit at the Ministry of Justice has produced several guidance notes for staff working with restricted patients. These can be downloaded from *www.noms.justice.gov.uk/news-publications-events/publications* (key word search for 'MHU'). They include:

- *Notes for the Guidance of Social Supervisors Mental Health Act 1983 Supervision and Aftercare of Conditionally Discharged Restricted Patients* (June 2007)

- *Notes for the Guidance of Supervising Psychiatrists Mental Health Act 1983 Supervision and Aftercare of Conditionally Discharged Restricted Patients* (June 2006)

- *Guidance for Responsible Medical Officers: Leave of Absence for Patients Subject to Restrictions* (March 2008)

Also available from the Department of Health at *www.dh.gov.uk* (search under 'gateway 8664'): *Procedure for the Transfer of Prisoners to and from Hospital under Sections 47 and 48 of the Mental Health Act 1983* (December 2007)

Facts

During the year 2006, there were 1,440 admissions to hospital of restricted patients. On any one day, there are approximately 3,601 restricted patients detained in hospitals across England and Wales[5]. The majority of restricted patients are male (3,159) and 21% of them (650) are held in the high secure hospitals (Broadmoor, Ashworth and Rampton).

Note

Section 45A (hospital direction with limitation direction), which was added to the Act via the Crime (Sentences) Act 1997, is not detailed in the following pages. This is because it is rarely used (four times during 2006 [5]), Section 45A is a court sentence to hospital for someone with a mental disorder. At any time after admission, if the responsible clinician considers that treatment is no longer required or beneficial, the person can be transferred back to prison to serve the remainder of their sentence. On admission to hospital it operates like a Section 47/49.

SECTION 37/41
HOSPITAL ORDER WITH RESTRICTION

Summary   A Crown Court orders (sentences) a person (under Section 37) to hospital for treatment and in order to protect the public from serious harm, restrictions are applied to the Section 37 using the power contained in Section 41. Consequently, the sections combine to produce Section 37/41.

Legal criteria

Crown Court: a person is convicted of an offence punishable with imprisonment

and the person is suffering from *mental disorder*

and the mental disorder is of a *nature or degree* which makes it appropriate for them to be detained in hospital for treatment

and *appropriate medical treatment is available*

and the court is of the opinion that the most suitable method of dealing with the person is by means of this order (Section 37)

and having regard to the nature of the offence, the offender's previous criminal record and the risk of them committing further offences if released, it is necessary for the protection of the public from serious harm for special restrictions to apply (Section 41 restriction).

The words in italics are defined on page 154

Powers   • *Detention* – the power to detain the person indefinitely.

• *Treatment* – the person can be given treatment for mental disorder with or without their consent (see page 79).

• *Absconding* – if the person absconds they can be forcibly returned to hospital by any authorised member of hospital staff or by the police. The Ministry of Justice should be informed immediately.

Who is involved?   *Two doctors,* one of whom must be Section 12 approved (have experience of psychiatry) or have approved clinician status. One of these doctors must give oral evidence before the court, preferably a doctor from the hospital the person will be sent to. The doctors may work for the same NHS Trust.
and
the *Crown Court* makes the order.

Time limits   The person must be admitted to hospital within 28 days of the order being made. If they are not admitted immediately, they can be detained for up to 28 days in a place of safety (for example prison) whilst a hospital bed is arranged.

Leave of absence	The authority to grant leave rests with the Ministry of Justice who produce an application form for responsible clinicians to request leave. The Ministry of Justice normally requires three weeks to consider a request for leave.

Escorted leave for a person to attend court for an alleged or proven offence or to attend another hospital for urgent medical treatment does not require prior Ministry of Justice approval, however they should be informed as soon as possible. |
| **Patient rights** | Appeals
The right of appeal to the Mental Health Review Tribunal but only in the second six months of detention and then once a year.

The right of appeal to the Hospital Managers, however they cannot discharge the person but only recommend discharge to the Ministry of Justice.

The right of appeal to the Crown Court or Court of Appeal to have the conviction quashed or another sentence imposed.

Advocacy
The right to an independent mental health advocate (IMHA).

Mental Health Act Commission/Care Quality Commission
The right to be visited by and complain to the Mental Health Act Commission/ Care Quality Commission. |
| **Duties on staff** | Staff should take all practicable steps to ensure the patient understands their legal rights and provide this information both orally and in writing (the Department of Health standard rights leaflets and a Ministry of Justice letter addressed to the person).

The responsible clinician must provide yearly reports to the Ministry of Justice.

The Ministry of Justice must refer the patient to a Mental Health Review Tribunal if their case has not been considered by the Tribunal in the previous three years (or one year if under 18).

The provision of after-care services under Section 117 upon discharge. |
| **Discharge** | There are a number of ways for the section to end:

Note: The majority of Section 37/41 orders are 'conditionally' discharged first before absolute discharge at a later date. This means the Section 37 ends but the Section 41 remains in place (see page 69).

❖ Discharge by a Mental Health Review Tribunal (conditional or absolute)

❖ Discharge by the Ministry of Justice, usually at the request of the responsible clinician (conditional or absolute)

❖ Discharge by the Crown Court or Court of Appeal (this may result in the person being sentenced again but under criminal law)

❖ A restriction order with a fixed time period expires. The section then becomes a normal Section 37 and begins from the date that the restriction order ends. Note: from 1st October 2007 all new restriction orders have no time period for expiry (without limit of time). |
| **Renewing the section** | It is not possible to renew the section because it is either set for a fixed period of time (like a prison sentence) or has no expiry date. |

Forms	The Crown Court issues a Section 37/41 order.
Facts	During 2006, Section 37/41 was used to admit 303 people to hospital[5].
Practical advice	A Magistrates' Court cannot make a Section 41 order, however, if it is making a Section 37 order and feels that a Section 41 is also required, it can transfer the case to a Crown Court.
Case Law	When the doctors give the court their evidence (opinion) as to why a restriction order is necessary, they should in particular clearly state why the order is necessary to protect the public from harm.
	From the case of R v Chalk [2002] EWCA
	The harm includes both physical and serious psychological harm.
	From the case of R v Melbourne [2000] CA
Mental Health Act 2007	The 2007 Act made a number of changes to Section 37/41:
	• All new restriction orders are now without limit of time
	• The single definition of mental disorder
	• The introduction of approved and responsible clinicians
	• The additional detention criteria that appropriate medical treatment must be available
	• Changes to the treatment powers of the Act
	• The right to an independent mental health advocate (IMHA)
	• Changes to the automatic referral periods for Tribunal hearings

SECTION 41
THE CONDITIONALLY DISCHARGED PATIENT

Summary
Section 41 operates like a community section for people who were originally on Section 37/41. When a Section 37/41 is conditionally discharged, it leaves the power of Section 41 in place. This means that the person can leave hospital and live in the community but with a number of conditions placed upon them. The section lasts for as long as the period of the original restriction order.

Legal criteria

Section 37/41 criteria (see page 55)

and the section is conditionally discharged by a
Mental Health Review Tribunal or the Ministry of Justice.

Powers
The powers are flexible but generally include:

- *Residence* – the person is required to live at a specified place. However, they are not detained there.

- *Treatment* – the person is required to accept treatment. However, they can only be given treatment with their consent.

- *Supervision* – to keep appointments and allow access to a supervisor (normally an approved mental health professional or probation officer) and a responsible clinician.

Failure to comply with the requirements of the order would lead to the Ministry of Justice being informed and the person could then be recalled to hospital. This would re-instate the powers of the original Section 37/41. During 2006, a total of 196 conditionally discharged people were recalled to hospital [5].

Who is involved?
The *Ministry of Justice* or *Mental Health Review Tribunal* instigates the order by discharging Section 37 from a Section 37/41. They then impose a number of conditions on the person under the power of the remaining Section 41.
and
a *community supervisor* will be appointed for the person (usually an approved mental health professional or probation officer). A responsible clinician will also be involved in monitoring the person in the community.

Time limits
The section lasts for as long as the original Section 41 order. This could be for an indefinite period of time. Note: from 1st October 2007 all new restriction orders have no time period for expiry (without limit of time).

Leave of absence
If the person is required to live at specified premises they need permission from the Ministry of Justice to move or to take leave from this place.

Patient rights
Appeals
The right of appeal to the Mental Health Review Tribunal once during the first 12 to 24 months after the conditional discharge and then once in every subsequent two year period.

No right of appeal to the Hospital Managers.

Advocacy
The right to an independent mental health advocate (IMHA).

Working With The Mental Health Act

Mental Health Act Commission/Care Quality Commission
The right to be visited by and complain to the Mental Health Act Commission/ Care Quality Commission.

Duties on staff	Although there is no specific rights leaflet for people who are conditionally discharged, staff should inform people of their rights under this section. The community supervisor and responsible clinician must provide reports to the Ministry of Justice on a regular basis.
Discharge	There are two ways for the section to end: ❖ Absolute discharge by the Mental Health Review Tribunal ❖ Absolute discharge by the Ministry of Justice
Renewing the section	It is not possible to renew the section because it lasts for a fixed or indefinite period of time dictated by the Section 41 restriction.
Forms	A conditional discharge order from either the Ministry of Justice or Mental Health Review Tribunal.
Practical advice	The Ministry of Justice, under guidance from the community supervisor and the responsible clinician, can recall the conditional discharge and the person would be re-admitted to hospital under the original powers of the Section 37/41. Once recalled, the Ministry of Justice must refer the person's case for a Mental Health Review Tribunal hearing within a month of their admission to hospital. The person can also be admitted to hospital as a voluntary patient or placed under a Section 2 or 3. In the event of such an admission to hospital, the responsible clinician must notify the Ministry of Justice promptly. The Ministry of Justice produces specific guidance on the supervision of conditionally discharged patients (see page 64).
Facts	360 people were conditionally discharged during 2006. The Mental Health Review Tribunal accounted for 309 of these conditional discharges whilst the Ministry of Justice agreed to 51 conditional discharges[5].
Mental Health Act 2007	The 2007 Act made the following changes to Section 41: ▪ The introduction of responsible clinicians and approved clinicians ▪ The right to an independent mental health advocate (IMHA) ▪ All new restriction orders are made without limit of time

Summary

The transfer of a sentenced prisoner to hospital and their detention there (Section 47) with restrictions applied (Section 49) by the Ministry of Justice. The Ministry produces a guide to the use of this power (see page 64).

Legal criteria

The person is serving a sentence of imprisonment
and the Secretary of State is satisfied they are suffering from *mental disorder*

and the mental disorder is of a *nature or degree* which makes it appropriate for them to be detained in hospital for medical treatment

and *appropriate medical treatment is available*

and the Secretary of State, having regard to the public interest and all the circumstances, may direct that the person is removed to and detained in hospital (Section 47)

and having regard to the nature of the offence, the previous criminal record of the offender and the risk of them committing further offences if released, that it is necessary for the protection of the public from serious harm for special restrictions to apply (Section 49).

The words in italics are defined on page 154

Powers

• *Detention* – the power to detain the person for as long as the restriction order is in place (that is the earliest date on which the prisoner may be discharged from prison) and thereafter as long as the Section 47 is in place.

• *Treatment* – the person can be given treatment for mental disorder with or without their consent (see page 79).

• *Absconding* – if the person absconds they can be forcibly returned to hospital by any authorised member of hospital staff or by the police. The Ministry of Justice must be informed immediately.

Who is involved?

Two doctors, one of whom must be Section 12 approved (have experience of psychiatry) or have approved clinician status. Both doctors may work for the same NHS Trust
and
the *Ministry of Justice* which agrees and issues the transfer direction.

The Ministry of Justice is not obliged to agree to a Section 47/49 despite two medical recommendations being made. It will consider whether the prisoner can be safely contained by the hospital taking into account a number of risk factors including the nature of the offence, the length of the sentence and the risk of absconding.

Time limits	The person must be admitted to hospital within 14 days of the Section 47/49 being made.
Leave of absence	The authority to grant leave rests with the Ministry of Justice and it will not normally be granted until the person is approaching their conditional, or non-parole, release date. Escorted leave for the person to attend court or to attend another hospital for urgent medical treatment does not require prior Ministry of Justice approval, however they should be informed.
Patient rights	Appeals The right of appeal to the Mental Health Review Tribunal once in the first six months, once during the second six months and thereafter yearly. The right of appeal to the Hospital Managers, without limit to the number of appeals, at the discretion of the Hospital Managers. However, they cannot discharge the person but only recommend discharge to the Ministry of Justice. Advocacy The right to an independent mental health advocate (IMHA). Mental Health Act Commission/Care Quality Commission The right to be visited by and complain to the Mental Health Act Commission/ Care Quality Commission.
Duties on staff	Staff should take all practicable steps to ensure the patient understands their legal rights and provide this information both orally and in writing (there is a standard Department of Health rights leaflet and a Ministry of Justice letter addressed to the person). The Ministry of Justice must refer the patient to the Mental Health Review Tribunal if their case has not been considered in the previous three years (or one year if under 18). The responsible clinician must provide annual reports to the Ministry of Justice. The provision of after-care services under Section 117 upon discharge.
Discharge	There are a number of ways for the section to end: ❖ Discharge by a Mental Health Review Tribunal (the person no longer requires treatment in hospital). The person would then return to prison unless the Ministry of Justice agreed to their discharge or the Tribunal ordered that they nonetheless remain in hospital. ❖ The responsible clinician notifies the Ministry of Justice that the person no longer requires treatment in hospital or that no effective treatment can be given. The Ministry of Justice may then return the person to prison, release them on parole or allow the discharge. ❖ If the person was subject to a fixed term sentence of imprisonment, the restriction (Section 49) will terminate on the person's release date. The person is then only subject to Section 47, which operates like a Section 37.
Renewing the section	It is not possible to renew the section because it runs for a fixed or indefinite period, set by the Section 49 restriction.

Forms	The Ministry of Justice issues a Section 47/49 transfer direction with restrictions.
Facts	Section 47/49 was used to transfer 421 people to hospital during 2006 [5].
Mental Health Act 2007	The 2007 Act made the following changes to Section 47/49: <ul><li>The single definition of mental disorder</li><li>The introduction of responsible clinicians and approved clinicians</li><li>The requirement that appropriate medical treatment be available</li><li>Changes to the treatment powers of the Act</li><li>The right to an independent mental health advocate (IMHA)</li><li>Changes to the automatic referral periods for Tribunals</li></ul>

74

Summary   The transfer of an unsentenced prisoner to hospital and their detention there (Section 48) with restrictions applied by the Ministry of Justice (Section 49). If the person is involved in criminal proceedings, a restriction order is mandatory but for other cases, the Ministry of Justice will make an individual assessment of risk. The Ministry produces a guide to the use of this power (see page 64).

Legal criteria

An unsentenced prisoner who is either detained in prison or a remand centre, or remanded in custody by a Magistrates' Court, or committed to prison by a court for a limited term, or detained under the Immigration Act 1971 or Section 62 of the Nationality, Immigration and Asylum Act 2002

and the Secretary of State is satisfied that the person is suffering from *mental disorder* of a *nature or degree* which makes it appropriate for them to be detained and treated in hospital

and *appropriate medical treatment is available*

and the person is in urgent need of such treatment (Section 48)

and having regard to the nature of the offence, the previous criminal record of the offender and the risk of them committing further offences if released, it is necessary for the protection of the public from serious harm for special restrictions to apply (Section 49).

The words in italics are defined on page 154

Powers
- *Detention* – the power to detain the person for a period of time as given by the restriction order.

- *Treatment* – the person can be given treatment for mental disorder with or without their consent (see page 79).

- *Absconding* – if the person absconds they can be forcibly returned to hospital by any authorised member of hospital staff or by the police. The Ministry of Justice must be informed immediately.

Who is involved?   *Two doctors,* one of whom must be Section 12 approved (have experience of psychiatry) or have approved clinician status. Both doctors may work for the same NHS Trust
and
the *Ministry of Justice* which agrees and issues the transfer direction.

It is important to note that the Ministry of Justice is not obliged to agree to a Section 48/49 despite two medical recommendations being made. It will consider whether the prisoner can be safely contained by the hospital, taking into account a number of risk factors including the nature of the offence, their behaviour in prison and the risk of absconding.

Working With The Mental Health Act

Time limits	The person must be admitted to hospital within 14 days of the Section 48/49 being issued.
Leave of absence	The authority to grant leave rests with the Ministry of Justice. Leave is not normally granted unless there are exceptional grounds for doing so. Escorted leave for a person to attend court for an alleged or proven offence or to attend another hospital for urgent medical treatment does not require prior Ministry of Justice approval, however they should be informed as soon as possible.
Patient rights	Appeals The right of appeal to the Mental Health Review Tribunal, once in the first six months, once in the second six months and thereafter yearly. The right of appeal to the Hospital Managers, without limit to the number of appeals, at the discretion of the Hospital Managers. However, they cannot discharge the person but only recommend discharge to the Ministry of Justice. Advocacy The right to an independent mental health advocate (IMHA). Mental Health Act Commission/Care Quality Commission The right to be visited by and complain to the Mental Health Act Commission/ Care Quality Commission.
Duties on staff	Staff should take all practicable steps to ensure the patient understands their legal rights and provide this information both orally and in writing (there is a standard Department of Health rights leaflet and a Ministry of Justice letter addressed to the person). The Ministry of Justice must refer the patient to the Mental Health Review Tribunal if their case has not been considered in the previous three years (or one year if under 18). The responsible clinician must provide annual reports to the Ministry of Justice. The provision of after-care services under Section 117 upon discharge.
Discharge	There are a number of ways for the section to end: ❖ When the court proceedings in connection with the section are complete. ❖ For patients under Section 48/49 remanded in custody by a Magistrates' Court, the restriction order ends at the expiration of the period of remand unless the person is then committed in custody to the Crown Court. ❖ For patients under Section 48/49 who are civil prisoners or immigration detainees the section ends on the expiration of the original detention period. ❖ Discharge by a Mental Health Review Tribunal. The person will then be detained under the criminal justice system as before, while the court considers the next course of action. ❖ If the responsible clinician reports to the Ministry of Justice that the person no longer requires treatment in hospital or that no effective treatment can be given, the person will be detained under the criminal justice system as before.
Renewing the section	The section can only be renewed if the court imposes another section on the person (Section 37 or 37/41) at the end of the trial.

Forms	The Ministry of Justice issues a Section 48/49 transfer direction order with restrictions.
Facts	473 people were transferred to hospital under Section 48/49 during 2006, making this the most used restricted section[5].
Mental Health Act 2007	The 2007 Act made the following changes to Section 48/49: • The single definition of mental disorder • The introduction of responsible clinicians and approved clinicians • The requirement that appropriate medical treatment be available • Changes to the treatment powers of the Act • The right to an independent mental health advocate (IMHA) • Changes to the automatic referral periods for Tribunals

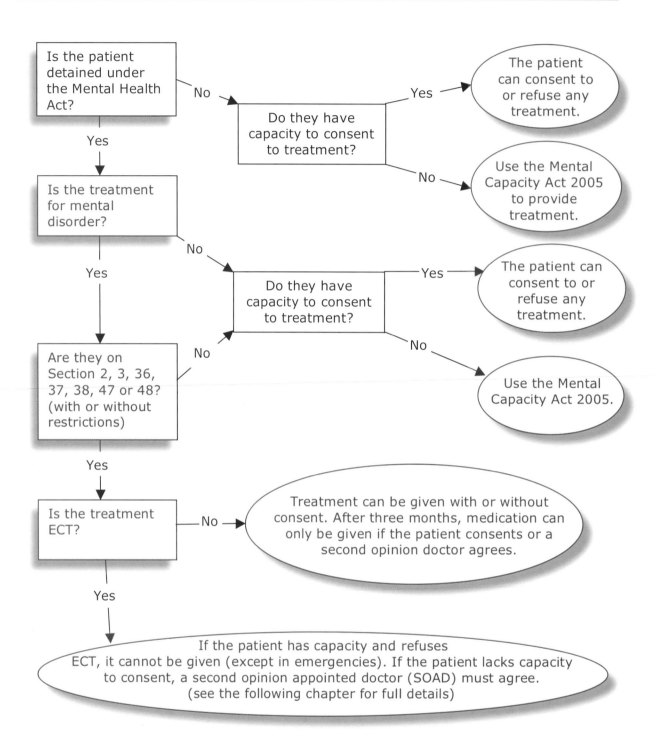

Note: If neurosurgery or the implantation of hormones is the proposed treatment, Section 57 will apply and the patient must consent and a second opinion doctor plus two other independent people must also agree. This applies to both detained and informal (voluntary) patients.

Community Treatment Orders – have separate treatment rules (see page 85).

The power to give treatment with or without consent is contained in Part 4 of the Act (*Consent to Treatment*). Sections 56 to 64, within Part 4, detail the powers available to treat people under the Act and the rules and limitations that apply to these powers.

The meaning of 'treatment'

Before considering the rules relating to the provision of treatment under the Act, it is important to look at the Act's definition of treatment. The majority of long-term detention sections (3, 36, 37, 37/41, 47, 47/49, 48, 48/49 and community treatment orders) require that *'appropriate medical treatment is available'* as one of the criteria for detention.

The phrase *'appropriate medical treatment is available'* can be split into four components which must all be met.

Appropriate = Medical treatment which is appropriate in the individual patient's case, taking into account the nature and degree of the mental disorder and all other circumstances of their case. This should include consideration of issues such as the patient's culture, ethnicity, religion, age, gender, family and social relationships as appropriate for the patient concerned. The Code of Practice states that any treatments which require the patient's co-operation to be effective are not inappropriate simply because a patient does not wish to engage with them.

Medical treatment = Medical treatment for mental disorder is defined by the Act (Section 145) and it includes nursing care, psychological intervention and specialist mental health habilitation, rehabilitation and care. This allows a broad range of treatments including medication, care to alleviate the symptoms of the disorder, nursing care, monitoring blood where this is part of taking certain medication, diagnostic tests for mental disorder and the care provided whilst a patient is in seclusion. General medical treatment may also be given if it can be shown to be treating a symptom directly resulting from the patient's mental disorder or integral to it. For example, the use of nasal-gastric tube feeding in the case of a patient with anorexia nervosa.

Treatment = The word treatment is further defined in the Act and means treatment *'the purpose of which is to alleviate or prevent a worsening of, the disorder or one or more of its symptoms or manifestations'*. The Code of Practice notes that *'Medical treatment may be for the purpose of alleviating, or preventing a worsening of, a mental disorder even though it cannot be shown in advance that any particular effect is likely to be achieved'*. Symptoms and manifestations can mean the way a disorder is experienced by the patient and how it manifests itself in the person's thoughts, emotions, communication, behaviour and actions.

Available = The treatment must be available to the patient. It is not sufficient that appropriate treatment could theoretically be provided. The Code states however that, *'...available treatment need not be the most appropriate medical treatment that could ideally be made available. Nor does it need to address every aspect of the person's disorder.'*

Therefore, for a person to be detained under the Act, where the criteria states *'appropriate medical treatment is available'* all four elements above must be satisfied. If they are not met, a person cannot be detained where this is a part of the detention criteria applicable to their section.

Medication and any other treatment in the first three months of detention (excluding ECT, neurosurgery or the implantation of hormones) (Section 63)

Section 63 of the Act provides the power to give treatment to detained patients with or without their consent in the first three months starting with the first time they are given medication (or other treatment).

Limitations

The key limitations on this power are:

- Only patients on long-term sections can be given such treatment (Sections 2, 3, 36, 37, 38, 47 and 48 (with or without restrictions).

- Patients under Sections 4, 5(2), 5(4), 35, 135(1), 136, guardianship or conditionally discharged (41 only) are not covered by this part of the Act and can only be given treatment if they have capacity and consent or, if they lack capacity, under the powers of the Mental Capacity Act.

- Community patients (those under community treatment orders) are not covered by Section 63. Separate powers are available for the treatment of community patients (see page 85).

- Treatment is only for mental disorder. Section 63 only includes physical treatment in so far as it can be shown to treat a symptom resulting directly from the patient's mental disorder or integral to it.

- Some treatments are excluded – electro convulsive therapy (ECT), neurosurgery and the surgical implantation of hormones.

- For medication, the power lasts for three months. After this, Section 58 applies – see next page.

Three month period

Although the three month period should begin when medication is first given, it is common practice to start it from the time a person is detained (not including the short-term sections listed earlier that are excluded from this part of the Act), which may be an earlier date than when the medication began.

Code of Practice

Although the Mental Health Act permits some medical treatment for mental disorder to be given without consent, the patient's consent should still be sought before treatment is given, wherever practicable. The patient's consent or refusal should be recorded in their notes, as should the treating clinician's assessment of the patient's capacity to consent.

Patients on leave

Patients detained under a relevant section to which the treatment powers apply but granted leave of absence are still covered by the treatment powers of the Act so the rules and procedures as given above apply to them in the same way.

After medication has been given for three months (under the powers of Section 63 above) Section 58 comes into force. This provides a form of protection for patients still being treated.

If the patient has capacity and consents to treatment, the responsible clinician must complete Form T2 stating that the patient has understood the nature, purpose and likely effects of the treatment and consented to it.

If the patient refuses treatment or does not have capacity to consent to it a second opinion appointed doctor must be called. They will consult a nurse who has been involved with the patient, another professional (not a nurse or doctor), the responsible clinician and the patient. Following these consultations, the second opinion appointed doctor can authorise the treatment if they consider it is appropriate for the treatment to be given (Form T3).

The three month period includes any time the patient was subject to a community treatment order.

Consent

Consent must be given freely, without coercion, threat or undue pressure. Whether a person has capacity to consent to treatment is assessed by using the test of capacity contained within the Mental Capacity Act 2005. The Code of Practice states that when obtaining consent, patients should be told that they may withdraw consent at any time.

Withdrawing consent

A patient may initially consent to treatment and a Form T2 is signed. However, consent is a continuing process and the patient may later refuse treatment. This would invalidate the form and the treatment must stop. A second opinion appointed doctor should then be called in order to authorise the treatment. If needed, during the interim period, emergency treatment may be considered under Section 62.

Form T2 would also become invalid if the person lost their capacity to consent to treatment or if the treatment prescribed was different to that originally written on the form. The reverse would also be true. If a person lacked capacity at the beginning of the treatment and then regained capacity during treatment, their consent must be sought.

Patients on leave

Patients detained under a relevant section to which the treatment powers apply but granted leave of absence under Section 17 are still covered by the treatment powers of the Act so the rules and procedures as given above apply to them in the same way.

- This power applies to patients on long-term sections (Sections 2, 3, 36, 37, 38, 47 and 48 with or without restrictions).

- Patients under 18 who are NOT detained are also covered by the legal criteria with special rules being applied (see the diagram on the next page for details).

- Community patients can also be given ECT but only if they consent unless they are recalled to hospital, in which case, their refusal of consent may be overridden. If they lack capacity to consent, they can be given ECT without the need for recall. However, in either situation, a certificate from a second opinion appointed doctor is required under Part 4A before ECT can be provided (see page 85).

- Patients under Sections 4, 5(2), 5(4), 35, 135(1), 136, guardianship or conditionally discharged (41 only) are not covered by this part of the Act and can only be given ECT if they have capacity and consent or, if they lack capacity, under the powers of the Mental Capacity Act.

Legal criteria for giving ECT

A patient detained under the Act can only be given ECT if they meet one of the following three criteria:

1) They are aged 18 or over
   and
   have consented to the treatment in question
   and
   either the approved clinician in charge **or** a second opinion appointed doctor has certified in writing that the patient is capable of understanding the nature, purpose and likely effects of the treatment and has consented to it (Form T4).

Therefore a detained patient with capacity can refuse ECT, however this can be overridden in an emergency under Section 62 (see page 84).

2) They are under 18
   and
   have consented to the treatment in question
   and
   a second opinion appointed doctor has certified in writing that the patient is capable of understanding the nature, purpose and likely effects of the treatment and has consented to it and that it is appropriate for the treatment to be given (Form T5).

Therefore a detained patient under 18 can refuse ECT. Even if they consent, a second opinion appointed doctor must always be used. If the patient refuses ECT, it can only be given as an emergency treatment under Section 62 (see page 84).

3) They are an adult (or under 18) who lacks capacity to consent to ECT and a second opinion appointed doctor has certified in writing (Form T6) that:

   (a) they are not capable of understanding the nature, purpose and likely effects of the treatment **but**

   (b) it is appropriate for the treatment to be given **and**

   (c) giving them the treatment would not conflict with an advance decision which is valid and applicable, or a decision made by a lasting power of attorney or deputy or by the Court of Protection.

Therefore a person can make an advance decision to refuse ECT and it would have to be respected despite the person being detained under the Mental Health Act and lacking capacity to consent. However, this can be overridden if the treatment is classed as an emergency under Section 62 (see page 84).

Working With The Mental Health Act

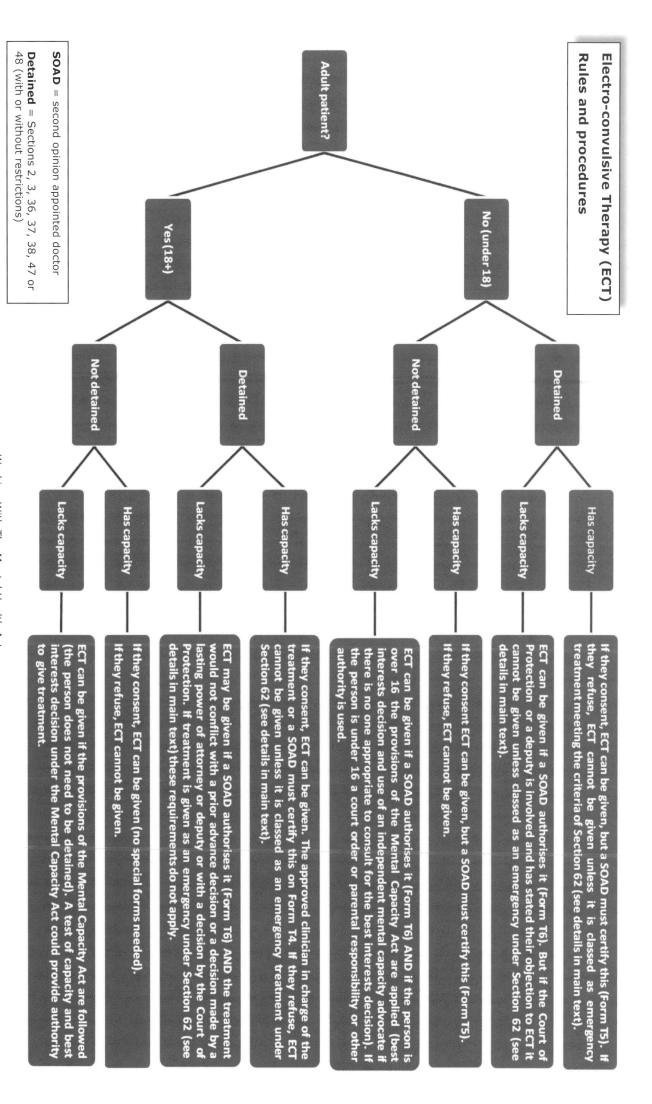

Electro-convulsive Therapy (ECT)
Rules and procedures

Adult patient?

Yes (18+)

No (under 18)

Not detained

Detained

Not detained

Detained

Lacks capacity

Has capacity

Lacks capacity

Has capacity

Lacks capacity

Has capacity

Lacks capacity

Has capacity

ECT can be given if the provisions of the Mental Capacity Act are followed (the person does not need to be detained). A test of capacity and best interests decision under the Mental Capacity Act could provide authority to give treatment.

If they consent, ECT can be given (no special forms needed).
If they refuse, ECT cannot be given.

ECT may be given if a SOAD authorises it (Form T6) AND the treatment would not conflict with a prior advance decision or a decision made by a lasting power of attorney or deputy or with a decision by the Court of Protection. If treatment is given as an emergency under Section 62 (see details in main text) these requirements do not apply.

If they consent, ECT can be given. The approved clinician in charge of the treatment or a SOAD must certify this on Form T4. If they refuse, ECT cannot be given unless it is classed as an emergency treatment under Section 62 (see details in main text).

ECT can be given if a SOAD authorises it (Form T6) AND if the person is over 16 the provisions of the Mental Capacity Act are applied (best interests decision and use of an independent mental capacity advocate if there is no one appropriate to consult for the best interests decision). If the person is under 16 a court order or parental responsibility or other authority is used.

If they consent ECT can be given, but a SOAD must certify this (Form T5).
If they refuse, ECT cannot be given.

ECT can be given if a SOAD authorises it (Form T6). But if the Court of Protection or a deputy is involved and has stated their objection to ECT it cannot be given unless classed as an emergency under Section 62 (see details in main text).

If they consent, ECT can be given, but a SOAD must certify this (Form T5). If they refuse, ECT cannot be given unless it is classed as emergency treatment meeting the criteria of Section 62 (see details in main text).

SOAD = second opinion appointed doctor
Detained = Sections 2, 3, 36, 37, 38, 47 or 48 (with or without restrictions)

Section 62 of the Act authorises the administration of treatment in circumstances where the procedures for Section 57 (special treatments), 58 (medication after three months) or 58A (ECT) cannot be followed because there is an urgent need to give the treatment.

- As with other treatment powers, Section 62 only relates to detained patients on long-term sections. There is no statutory form for using Section 62 so each NHS Trust can produce its own.

- Patients under Sections 4, 5(2), 5(4), 35, 135(1), 136, guardianship, or conditionally discharged (41 only) are not covered by this power. Special rules apply for people on community treatment orders (see page 85).

Legal criteria

Sections 62 (1) (a-d) define urgent treatment as:

(a) treatment which is immediately necessary to save the patient's life **or**

(b) treatment which (not being irreversible) is immediately necessary to prevent a serious deterioration of the patient's condition **or**

(c) treatment which (not being irreversible or hazardous) is immediately necessary to alleviate serious suffering to the patient **or**

(d) treatment which (not being irreversible or hazardous) is immediately necessary and represents the minimum interference necessary to prevent the patient from behaving violently or being a danger to themselves or to others.

In addition Section 62(2) states that where a patient has previously consented to treatment and then withdraws their consent, the treatment may be continued if the approved clinician considers that ceasing the treatment would cause serious suffering to the patient.

Electro-convulsive therapy

For ECT only the first two categories apply. Therefore, to be classed as urgent treatment under the Act, the ECT must be either:

- immediately necessary to save the patient's life **or**

- treatment which (not being irreversible) is immediately necessary to prevent a serious deterioration in the patient's condition.

Irreversible and hazardous

The Act defines 'irreversible' as treatment that has unfavourable irreversible physical or psychological consequences. 'Hazardous' is defined as treatment that entails significant physical hazard.

Practical advice

Section 62 is designed to allow emergency treatment in circumstances where the other treatment powers cannot be used. However, the other treatment powers of the Act should be brought into place swiftly to end the need for Section 62. For example, Section 62 may be needed when a patient who had consented to treatment under a Form T2 (medication after three months) then withdraws their consent. Whilst the responsible clinician waits for a second opinion appointed doctor to authorise continued treatment they may continue to give treatment under the powers of Section 62.

Patients subject to community treatment orders (known as community patients) are not included under the treatment rules of Part 4 (as given above) unless they are recalled to hospital, instead they are covered by Part 4A.

A community patient with capacity

A community patient with capacity to make treatment decisions that has not been recalled may not be given treatment unless they consent to that treatment. The position would be the same even if they needed emergency treatment for their mental disorder. However, if recalled, a community patient would then be subject to the rules of Part 4 in the same way as other detained patients.

A community patient lacking capacity to consent to treatment

A patient subject to a community treatment order that has not been recalled and lacks capacity to consent to treatment may be given treatment using the Act if:

1. they have an attorney or deputy who can give authority for the treatment. Or, if the Court of Protection is asked to give authority, through an order of the court
   or
2. it does not conflict with an advance decision made by the patient or the views of an attorney, deputy or the Court of Protection
   and
   there is no reason to believe that the patient would object to the treatment or, if there is a belief that the patient may object, it is not necessary to use any force in order to give the treatment against these objections.

The Code gives the following guidance to establish whether a patient objects to treatment:

'In many cases, patients will be perfectly able to state their objection either verbally or by their dissenting behaviour. But in other cases, especially where patients are unable to communicate (or only able to communicate to a limited extent), clinicians will need to consider the patient's behaviour, wishes, feelings, views, beliefs and values, both present and past, so far as they can be ascertained.

If there is a reason to think the patient would object, if able to do so, then the patient should be taken to be objecting'.

Part 4A certificates

Community patients need a certificate from a second opinion appointed doctor regardless of their consent, for medication after one month and for ECT at any time. Medication can be given during the first month of a community treatment order without a certificate but after this period, one must be in place (Form CTO11) for medication to continue.

Example: Sarah is detained under Section 3 and given treatment immediately. After three months, she consents to further medication and her approved clinician completes Form T2. After a further four months, she is discharged from detention subject to a community treatment order. Once in the community, she is now subject to the Part 4A treatment rules. Treatment continues with her consent but a Part 4A certificate (Form CTO11 from a second opinion appointed doctor) will be required one month from when the community treatment order begins.

Emergency treatment

Community patients that lack capacity may be given emergency treatment under Section 64G if it is immediately necessary. Treatment is considered immediately necessary if it falls within any of the categories of 64G (a) to (d). These are the same as Sections 62 (1) (a) to (d) already given above.

If the proposed emergency treatment is ECT, it can only be given under Sections 64G (5) (a) or (b) (these are the same as Sections 62 (1) (a) or (b) above).

Emergency treatment can be given even if it contradicts the refusal of an attorney, deputy or a decision of the Court of Protection.

Force can also be used in these circumstances even if it goes against any known objections. However, the force can only be used if it is necessary to prevent harm to the patient and the force used is proportionate to the likelihood of that harm and the seriousness of that harm.

The Code of Practice states that force should only be used on community patients (patients subject to community treatment orders that have not been recalled) in exceptional cases.

Treatment under recall

When a patient under a community treatment order is recalled (72 hour maximum time period) the treatment rules under Part 4 apply during that period of recall – see above and also the diagram on page 87.

Treatment of children under a community treatment order

In terms of consent to treatment, the appropriate term for those under 16 years of age is 'competence'. In order to decide whether a child is competent to consent to treatment, the provisions of relevant children's legislation must be applied instead (see page 137).

Children (under 16) who are competent to consent

The rules governing the treatment of community patients under 16 that have not been recalled to hospital are contained within Section 64E of the Act. The person must consent and there must be authority to give the proposed treatment and if the treatment is provided after one month (this period begins with the day on which the community treatment order is made) or is ECT, a certificate must also be provided by a second opinion appointed doctor. There is no requirement for a certificate in emergencies.

Children who lack competence to consent

For community patients under 16 lacking competence to consent to the treatment, the relevant provisions are contained within Section 64F. If treatment is being given under Section 64F, the following criteria must be satisfied:

> The child's competence to consent has been assessed
> **and**
> it is reasonable to believe that the child does lack competence to consent
> **and**
> there is no reason to believe the child objects to the treatment
> **or**
> there is reason to believe the child objects but it will not be necessary to use force against these objections to give treatment
> **and**
> treatment is being given by or under the direction of the approved clinician.

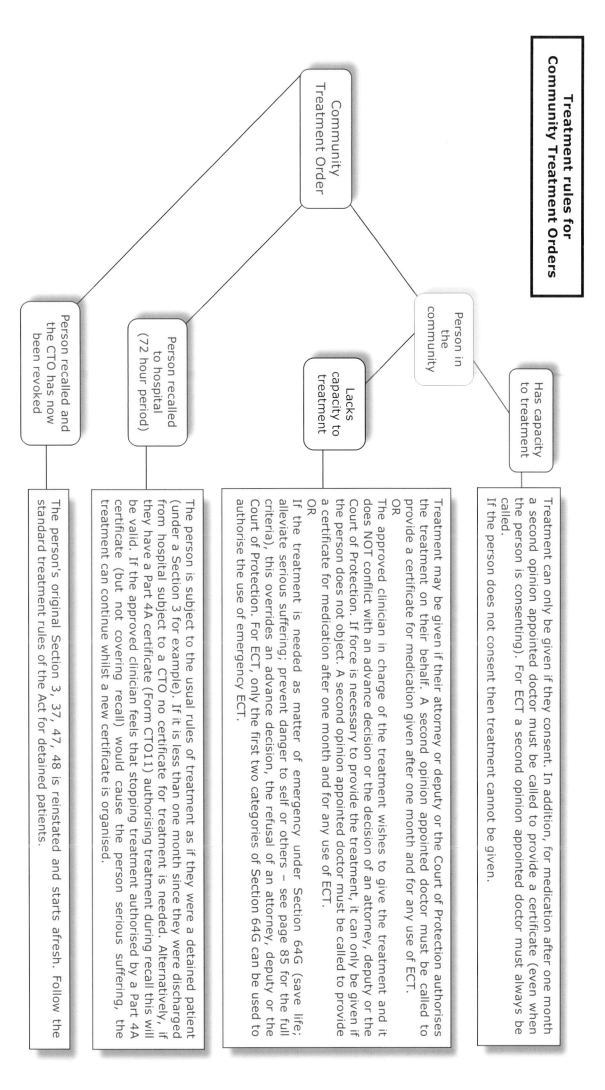

**Community
Treatment Order**

**Person in
the
community**

**Has capacity
to treatment**

Treatment can only be given if they consent. In addition, for medication after one month a second opinion appointed doctor must be called to provide a certificate (even when the person is consenting). For ECT a second opinion appointed doctor must always be called.

If the person does not consent then treatment cannot be given.

**Lacks
capacity to
treatment**

Treatment may be given if their attorney or deputy or the Court of Protection authorises the treatment on their behalf. A second opinion appointed doctor must be called to provide a certificate for medication given after one month and for any use of ECT.
OR
The approved clinician in charge of the treatment wishes to give the treatment and it does NOT conflict with an advance decision or the decision of an attorney, deputy or the Court of Protection. If force is necessary to provide the treatment, it can only be given if the person does not object. A second opinion appointed doctor must be called to provide a certificate for medication after one month and for any use of ECT.
OR
If the treatment is needed as matter of emergency under Section 64G (save life; alleviate serious suffering; prevent danger to self or others – see page 85 for the full criteria), this overrides an advance decision, the refusal of an attorney, deputy or the Court of Protection. For ECT, only the first two categories of Section 64G can be used to authorise the use of emergency ECT.

**Person recalled
to hospital
(72 hour period)**

The person is subject to the usual rules of treatment as if they were a detained patient (under a Section 3 for example). If it is less than one month since they were discharged from hospital subject to a CTO no certificate for treatment is needed. Alternatively, if they have a Part 4A certificate (Form CTO11) authorising treatment during recall this will be valid. If the approved clinician feels that stopping treatment authorised by a Part 4A certificate (but not covering recall) would cause the person serious suffering, the treatment can continue whilst a new certificate is organised.

**Person recalled and
the CTO has now
been revoked**

The person's original Section 3, 37, 47, 48 is reinstated and starts afresh. Follow the standard treatment rules of the Act for detained patients.

Neurosurgery and the implantation of hormones (Section 57)

Section 57 of the Act concerns special treatments that require additional procedures to be followed before they can be given. In contrast to the other treatment rules (except ECT for those under 18), this section applies to all patients, detained or informal (voluntary). The special treatments are:

- surgery to destroy brain tissue or the functioning of brain tissue (neurosurgery).

- other treatment as specified by regulations made by the Secretary of State for Health. To date this has been the surgical implantation of hormones to reduce male sex drive.

To carry out either of the above treatments the patient MUST consent and a second opinion appointed doctor and two other independent people (appointed by the Mental Health Act Commission) must agree that the patient has capacity to consent to the treatment. In addition, the second opinion appointed doctor must consult with two members of staff involved in the patient's treatment (one nurse and one other professional who is not a nurse or doctor) before agreeing that the treatment should be given (Form T1).

Approved clinicians

In certain circumstances, approved clinicians must be in charge of the treatment.

Patients detained under Sections 2, 3, 37, 47 and 48 (with or without restrictions):

- where the patient does not consent
- if the treatment is being given under Section 58 or 58A with a certificate by an approved clinician instead of an second opinion appointed doctor
- where the treatment is being continued for a community patient that has been recalled to hospital

Community treatment orders:

If the treatment is being given to a patient that lacks capacity to consent to it and they do not have a deputy, attorney or Court of Protection decision agreeing to it.

Review of treatment (Section 61)

Section 61 places a duty on the responsible clinician to regularly review the treatment of patients for whom a second opinion appointed doctor has authorised treatment. The review requires the responsible clinician to complete Form MHAC1 whenever the patient's section is renewed, when requested by the Mental Health Act Commission/Care Quality Commission or, for restricted patients, six months after their section began and then yearly.

Treatment for children

In terms of consent to treatment, the appropriate term for those under 16 years of age is 'competence'. In order to decide whether a child is competent to consent to treatment, the provisions of relevant children's legislation must be applied instead (see page 137).

Case Law

The courts have ruled that if a person with the mental capacity to refuse treatment is detained under the Mental Health Act, treatment for mental disorder can be given without their consent. Such treatment does not conflict with the Human Rights Act.

In the case concerned, PS was detained in hospital under the Act. It was accepted that he had capacity to give or withhold consent to treatment. PS argued that compulsory treatment would breach the prohibition on torture and inhuman and degrading treatment under Article 3 of the European Convention on Human Rights and his right to respect his private life under Article 8.

However, the court did not agree and stated that mental capacity is only one of the factors to be taken into account when deciding what is medically necessary and in the best interests of the patient. Therefore, a competent *detained* patient can be forced to accept medical treatment for mental disorder even if they oppose the treatment.

(From the case of: R (on the application of PS) v (1) Dr G and (2) Dr W [2003] EWHC 2335 (Admin), September 2003)

Further information

The Mental Health Act Commission/Care Quality Commission has produced a number of guidance notes concerning treatment (see page 148).

The Mental Health Act 2007

The impact of the 2007 Act was considerable on this part of the legislation:

- The removal of the previous 'treatability test' in the Act and its replacement with the requirement that appropriate medical treatment be available for a patient
- Additional protection given to young people under 18 for certain treatments
- Rules on ECT changed, allowing detained patients to refuse it and recognising advance decisions
- A series of new rules in relation to people on community treatment orders
- The use of the term 'capacity' to consent to treatment as defined by the Mental Capacity Act 2005
- The introduction of approved and responsible clinicians

A detained patient may not leave hospital unless granted leave under Section 17 of the Act (or Section 19 if being transferred to another hospital).

Rules

- A responsible clinician may grant leave to patients on Section 2, 3, 37, 47 or 48.

- A responsible clinician cannot grant leave to patients on Section 35, 36 or 38.

- The leave may be granted with or without conditions, as considered appropriate by the responsible clinician, in the interests of the patient or for the protection of others.

- For patients detained under Section 3, 37, 47 or 48 leave over seven consecutive days cannot be granted unless the responsible clinician has first considered whether the patient should be discharged under a community treatment order instead.

- The responsible clinician can require the patient to be escorted by another person during their leave for the protection of the patient or others. In this case, the patient can be escorted by a member of hospital staff or another person as authorised in writing by the responsible clinician.

- A responsible clinician may NOT grant leave to restricted patients without the prior approval of the Ministry of Justice. The Ministry produces specific guidance on this subject (see page 64).

There are no legal formalities applicable when a detained patient needs to go to a different part of the hospital or hospital grounds (except in the case of restricted patients required to stay in a particular part of the hospital). Such leave may be a useful part of the patient's care plan and may form part of the preparation to granting leave beyond the hospital grounds.

Extending leave

Leave may be extended in the absence of the patient, for a specified period. If the total amount of leave is over seven consecutive days, discharging the patient subject to a community treatment order must be considered first.

Length of leave

Leave can be granted for a specific period of time such as a weekend, or for a specific occasion such as a family celebration. The period of leave may also be undefined.

Code of Practice

- ➤ The responsible clinician cannot delegate the decision to grant leave. However, if the responsible clinician is absent, for example due to leave or illness, the approved clinician acting as the patient's responsible clinician at that time could grant the leave instead. The responsible clinician's consideration of granting long-term leave as opposed to a community treatment order should be recorded.

- ➤ The Hospital Managers cannot overrule a decision to grant leave.

- ➤ The responsible clinician must first establish whether accommodation or services are available to a patient before any conditions of leave are set.

> Voluntary patients (those not detained under the Act) may leave at any time. They do not need to request such leave but the Code advises they should inform staff.

Planning and consultation

The Code of Practice emphasises that leave should be well planned and provide an opportunity to assess how the patient would manage if discharged. The patient should be involved in the decision to grant leave and, with the patient's consent, relatives, carers and friends should be consulted, especially if the patient is to reside with them during their leave. A responsible clinician should carefully consider whether to grant leave if the patient does not consent to consultation with relatives, carers or friends who are to be involved in their care. The Code suggests that an up-to-date description of the patient is provided in the notes in case they do not return from their leave.

Short-term leave

The responsible clinician can grant short-term periods of leave. The times at which this leave is actually taken by the patient may be at the discretion of nursing staff. However, the leave must be taken within the period originally granted by the responsible clinician. The responsible clinician should continue to review the leave regularly and record this in the patient's notes.

Records

There is no statutory leave of absence form so each NHS Trust should produce one. A copy should be given to the patient and all those involved in their care.

Duty of care

The responsible clinician remains responsible for the patient's care and treatment while they are on leave. The duty to provide after-care services under Section 117 includes detained patients on leave.

The patient is still subject to the usual powers of detention while on leave. If a patient does not consent to medication while on leave, they can be recalled to hospital in order to administer medication under Part 4 of the Act (treatment powers). However, recall to provide medication is not a legal requirement.

Another hospital

Leave can also be used to allow a patient to stay in another hospital if required, for example for medical treatment. However, if such leave continues for an extended period of time, transfer of the patient to the other hospital should be considered (see page 109).

Case Law

A consultant's [now responsible clinician's] authority to grant leave does not extend to a duty upon the NHS to provide funding to facilitate the patient's use of their leave. A consultant will decide to grant leave of absence on the basis of the risk to the patient or others, they should not also have to consider financial constraints.

(From the case of: R v West London Mental Health NHS Trust 2006 (CA))

Further information

The Mental Health Act Commission/Care Quality Commission has produced a guidance note on leave (see page 148). The Ministry of Justice has also produced a guide to leave for people on forensic restricted sections (see page 64).

REVOKING LEAVE OF ABSENCE (RECALLING THE PATIENT)

A responsible clinician can revoke a patient's leave of absence under Section 17(4) if it is considered necessary in the interests of the patient's health or safety or for the protection of other people.

Procedure

- In order to recall a patient, notice in writing must be given to the patient or to the person in charge of the patient while they are on leave.

- The reasons for the recall should be explained to the patient and the explanation should be recorded in their notes.

Time limits

Leave of absence cannot be revoked if a person is no longer liable to be detained under the Act or has been on leave continuously for more than 12 months, whichever is earlier.

Recall of restricted patients

For patients on restricted Sections 37/41, 47/49 and 48/49 either a responsible clinician or the Ministry of Justice can revoke leave. However, the patient cannot be recalled if the period of detention has expired.

Code of Practice

Responsible clinicians must consider what effect being recalled may have on the patient. A refusal to take medication would not, on its own, be a reason for revocation, although it would almost always be a reason to consider revocation.

Relatives, carers, friends and professionals involved with the patient should contact the patient's responsible clinician if they believe the patient should return to hospital before their leave is due to end. The Code states that the responsible clinician should be easily accessible in order for this to happen.

Section 18 of the Act provides the power to retake a patient detained under the legislation who is absent without leave (AWOL).

Criteria

Detained patients will be considered absent without leave in the following circumstances:

> ➢ Leaving hospital without being granted leave

> ➢ Failing to return to hospital after a period of authorised leave has expired

> ➢ Failing to return to hospital after being recalled from a period of authorised leave

> ➢ Community patients that have been recalled and then abscond

> ➢ Community patients that do not return to hospital when recalled

> ➢ Being absent without authority from the address they are required to reside at, for example as a condition of their leave or under terms imposed by their guardian

> ➢ Conditionally discharged restricted patients who have been recalled to hospital and then abscond

> ➢ Additionally, the Code states that patients under Sections 135 and 136 can also be returned if they abscond from the place of safety at which they are being held. The same principle applies to patients that abscond while being conveyed and patients that are to be in the custody of an escort as a condition of their leave and abscond from that custody

Taking into custody

The following people can take a detained patient who is absent without leave into custody and return them to a specified address or hospital:

> ➢ An approved mental health professional
> ➢ A member of hospital staff (including staff of a hospital the patient is required to reside at as a condition of their leave - this must be authorised by the managers of the detaining hospital)
> ➢ A police officer
> ➢ A person authorised in writing by the Hospital Managers
> ➢ For guardianship the following people are authorised: responsible local authority (social services) staff, a police officer or any person authorised by the guardian or local authority.

Entering locked premises

Although the Act provides the legal authority to retake a detained patient who is absent without leave, the patient may be in private premises and prevent access. In these circumstances, staff would need to apply to a magistrate for a Section 135(2) warrant (see page 21). This provides the additional authority to forcibly enter private locked premises and retake a detained patient who is absent without leave.

Patients taken to another hospital

If a patient who is absent without leave is taken to another hospital, the hospital may be given the authority in writing by the original detaining hospital to detain the patient in the short-term until arrangements are made for their return. The Code states that this authority can be faxed or scanned until the original document is made available.

Patients subject to short-term powers

Patients who are absent without leave under one of the following short-term sections cannot be taken into custody if that section has expired – Sections 2, 4, 5(2), 5(4), 135(1) and 136.

Patients subject to long-term powers

Patients who are absent without leave and on Section 3, 7, 37 (both hospital order and guardianship order) 47 or a recalled community treatment order can be returned:

> ➢ up to six months after going absent without leave
> **or**
> ➢ until the expiry date of the section they are under

The later date of the above two will be the relevant date. If a person returns after being absent without leave for more than 28 days, a number of procedural steps have to be taken. For further details see the *Reference Guide to the Mental Health Act* available from the Department of Health[4]. The Act requires that the person is reassessed within one week of their return with a view to considering the need for continued detention. Form H6 or G10 (guardianship) or CTO8 (community treatment orders) must be completed as appropriate. If this is not done, the patient's detention or community treatment order will automatically end.

Patients subject to restriction orders

Patients on restricted Sections 37/41, 47/49 and 48/49 are not subject to time limits and can be retaken for as long as their section is in force. The Ministry of Justice must be informed immediately when any restricted patient goes absent without leave.

Retaking patients outside England and Wales

The Act allows for the retaking of patients while they are in any part of the United Kingdom, Isle of Man or Channel Islands. It applies only to patients who are absent without leave from a hospital in England and Wales.

Code of Practice

Hospitals should have clear policies relating to patients that are absent without leave. These policies should be agreed with other relevant agencies such as the police and ambulance services. The Code gives further detail as to what should be included in these policies.

The police should only be used to return a detained patient to hospital where necessary. Where the location of the patient is known, the role of the police should be to support the mental health staff in returning the patient.

The police should be informed immediately if a patient goes absent without leave who is particularly vulnerable, considered dangerous or under a restriction order.

Any incidence of absence without leave should be analysed with a view to avoiding a reoccurrence and also to applying conditions in the future.

If a patient is absent without leave for more than a few hours their nearest relative should be informed (subject to limitations of consulting with a nearest relative, see page 116).

Criminal offence

It is a criminal offence under Section 128 of the Act to induce or assist a person who is detained to go absent without leave from hospital. In addition, it is also an offence to knowingly hide a person who is absent without leave from hospital.

A patient wishing to appeal against their detention under the Act may do so in one of two ways:

> ➢ appeal to a Mental Health Review Tribunal (see page 100).
> **or**
> ➢ appeal to the Hospital Managers (see page 104).

As a general rule, patients on short-term detention sections (72 hours or less) do not have a right of appeal but most other patients do. To see which sections can be appealed against, please refer to the *Patient rights* segment in the chapters on detention sections.

Automatic appeals

One of the most important protective mechanisms within the Act is the automatic appeals process. The rules below detail when a patient will have their case automatically sent by the hospital to the Tribunal for an appeal hearing. The hearing will allow the Tribunal to consider whether the patient needs continued detention or in fact no longer meets the criteria for detention and should be discharged.

First six months of detention

A hospital will automatically send the case of a patient to the Tribunal after the first six months of detention under Section 3 (including any time spent under Section 2 immediately before this), unless any of the following circumstances apply:

- The patient appeals during that time themselves
- The patient's nearest relative appeals
- The case has been referred to a Tribunal by the Secretary of State

After three years of detention (or one year if the patient is under 18)

A patient will also be automatically referred for a Tribunal hearing if three years (or one year if the patient is under 18) have passed without the patient's case being heard by the Tribunal through any of the above methods. This includes patients on Sections 3, 37, 47, 48, 47/49 and 48/49.

Community treatment orders

The hospital will automatically refer the patient's case to the Tribunal in the following circumstances:

- If the patient's community treatment order is recalled and then revoked
- After the first six months of a community treatment order (or a combination of in-patient and community treatment order) if the patient has not had a hearing.
- After three years have passed without the patient having a further Tribunal hearing (for those under 18 the period is one year).

Special appeals

The Code of Practice states the Hospital Managers should ask the Secretary of State for Health to make an appeal for a Tribunal where the patient lacks the capacity to request a one and either the patient's case has never been considered by the Tribunal, or a significant period has passed since it was last considered.

The Code gives further examples where the Hospital Managers should consider such requests for hearings.

Withdrawing an appeal

If a patient wishes to withdraw their appeal after it has been made, they may do so by putting the request in writing. It is at the discretion of the Tribunal or the Hospital Managers as to whether they accept the withdrawal request. They may ask the patient's solicitor to confirm the details or may decide to proceed with the hearing regardless.

Location

Tribunal and Hospital Managers' hearings will normally be conducted in a room within the hospital grounds. The patient and ward will be notified of the time and location. Appropriate community settings may be used for patients subject to guardianship or community treatment orders.

Constitution

A Tribunal panel consists of three people:

- *President* – the person seated in the centre is the legal member and is called the president. They act much like a chairperson during the hearing.

- *Medical member* – the medical member is a consultant psychiatrist and will have already met with the patient prior to the hearing.

- *Lay member* – this person does not necessarily hold any legal or medical qualifications, however they should have general experience in mental health.

In Hospital Managers' hearings, the members (usually three but there may be more) are not required to have any medical or legal qualifications. They will be members of the organisation in charge of the hospital. In an NHS hospital, this could be the chair or non-executive directors of an NHS trust. Alternatively, they can be members of a committee or sub-committee authorised to carry out the work of the Hospital Managers. For independent hospitals, the Hospital Managers should not have a financial interest in the hospital or be a member of staff.

Nearest relative and carers

Nearest relatives have their own rights of appeal under the Act (see page 116).

With the patient's consent, their nearest relative should be informed of the hearing. Relatives, carers and friends may also be invited to the hearing to express their views to the panel. However, if the patient objects to this, an appropriate member of the professional team should be asked to incorporate these views into their report. The patient may invite anyone they choose to attend the hearing with them.

Reports

Before the hearing takes place, written reports should be produced. There is a legal duty to ensure reports are produced. The reports should be as current as possible to avoid the need for adjournment. The Tribunal may request supplementary reports if they need further evidence. Information about the style and content of reports can be found on page 106.

Procedure

The burden of proof is on the detaining authority. That is, they must prove their case – showing that the patient meets the detention criteria of the section they are subject to when the hearing is held.

Although the format of a hearing may vary, the following procedure is the general way in which hearings are conducted.

➢ Each person at the hearing, including the panel, will introduce themselves.

- The patient should be given the opportunity to explain their reasons for requesting discharge (if they have requested the discharge themselves).
- The patient should be allowed a friend or representative they have chosen to help and support them when they put their views to the panel.
- The responsible clinician and other professionals should explain why they believe the patient's continued detention is justified.
- All parties at the hearing (including the patient if they want this to be the case) should be able to hear each other's statements and to put questions to each other.
- The patient should be offered the opportunity of speaking to the panel in private.

The order of witnesses will usually be as follows:

- responsible clinician
- care co-ordinator or approved mental health professional
- nurse
- patient

Each witness will usually be asked to summarise their report and perhaps to provide an update if anything significant has happened since the report was written. They will then be asked to answer any questions the panel may have for them. Any questions that the patient or their legal representative has will then be put to each witness. Finally, a closing argument or speech is given by the patient or their legal representative before the panel retire to consider their verdict.

The Code of Practice notes that *'A responsible clinician can attend the hearing solely as a witness or as the nominated representative of the responsible authority. As a representative of the responsible authority, the responsible clinician has the ability to call and cross-examine witnesses and to make submissions to the Tribunal.'*

Etiquette

The appropriate form of address for the chairperson or president of a hearing is 'Sir' or 'Madam'. When a witness is giving evidence, the other witnesses should remain silent. The hearing itself is relatively informal, it is conducted while seated around a table and witnesses give evidence from their seats.

Legal representation

It should be noted that the style of advocacy used by legal representatives should not be adversarial as with most other legal hearings in this country. Instead, the purpose of the hearing is to get a balanced and accurate picture of the patient and therefore the advocacy should be conducted in an inquisitorial style. That is, the focus of all parties should be to establish the actual facts of the situation as objectively as possible, as opposed to trying to place blame on either party.

Patients are entitled to free legal representation at Tribunals regardless of their financial circumstances. Hospitals should ensure they have an up-to-date list of solicitors approved by the Law Society to represent patients at Tribunals. The Tribunal may adjourn a hearing where a patient is not legally represented and ask that such representation is organised to ensure the patient has the best opportunity to present their case. Automatic free legal representation at Hospital Managers' hearings is not available, however many solicitors offer such support and a patient should discuss this with their solicitor.

Code of Practice

Staff should encourage patients to attend hearings unless it would be detrimental to their health or well being.

All those attending hearings should be prepared to answer questions and give evidence to assist the hearing.

After-care arrangements

In the event of a Hospital Managers' or Tribunal hearing being minded to discharge a patient, they need to consider arrangements for their after-care following discharge. If these have yet to be made, it may be appropriate to adjourn for a brief period to allow for a Care Programme Approach (CPA) meeting to take place.

Delayed (deferred) discharge

A hearing may decide to order the delayed discharge of a patient. This can be used to allow arrangements to be made prior the patient being discharged, for example ensuring that appropriate after-care services will be available. A delayed discharge can state a specific date in the future when the patient will be discharged from section. For restricted forensic patients, the Tribunal can make a general requirement of conditions that must be met without a specific time limit attached, such as the provision of housing, before the discharge will take place.

The decision

In practice, in addition to the statutory criteria (see page 100), the panel's main concerns will be:

> ➢ Does the patient accept their condition and generally show insight into the mental disorder?
> ➢ Is the patient co-operative with mental health services and is their compliance likely to continue after discharge?
> ➢ Is the patient compliant with taking medication and is this likely to continue after discharge?
> ➢ Is there any distinction between what can be done for the patient in hospital or can they be as effectively treated in the community? (For example, with support from carers).

The decision of the panel and their reasons for it must be recorded and placed in the patient's records. The patient and all those attending the hearing should be informed of the decision in writing. The nearest relative should also be informed with the patient's consent. At least one member of the panel should meet with the patient to give them the decision in person and explain the reasoning behind it.

Appealing against the decision of a hearing

In order to appeal against a decision of the Tribunal (first-tier) an application should be made to the Upper Tribunal. In the case of the Hospital Managers, an application for judicial review must be made.

There is a right of appeal to the Mental Health Review Tribunal for many detained patients. A patient's nearest relative also has a separate right of appeal against the patient's detention in certain circumstances. In addition, hospitals and care homes that detain patients have a duty to refer cases to the Tribunal when a patient has not had a Tribunal hearing for a certain period of time (see the individual sections for further information and the previous chapter).

From 3rd November 2008, the Mental Health Review Tribunal was replaced by the First-tier Tribunal within the Health Education and Social Care chamber for Tribunals. It was renamed the *Mental Health Review Panel*. The change had little effect on hospitals and hearings remain the same as before. The new system however means that appeals against Panel decisions are now be made to an Upper Tribunal rather than through judicial review. The term *Tribunal* is used throughout this guide to refer to the Mental Health Review Panel as this is the name mental health staff are most familiar with.

Contact

Mental Health Review Tribunal/Panel
PO Box 8793, 5th Floor, Arnhem House, Leicester LE1 8BN

London & West: 0116 249 7068   *Midlands: 0116 249 7057*
South East & West: 0116 249 7019   *North: 0116 249 7051*

Website: www.tribunals.gov.uk

Facts

The Tribunal has a considerable workload. For the year ending March 2007, it received over 21,000 individual appeals/referrals. This resulted in 12,000 actual Tribunal hearings with a discharge rate of 16% [6].

Powers of Tribunals

Sections 72 to 74 of the Act give the criteria to be met before a Tribunal may discharge a patient. The discharge criteria vary in accordance with the section under which a patient is detained. The Tribunal makes its decisions based on the civil standard of proof, which is, on the *balance of probabilities*. In other words, what is more likely than not.

Procedure

At the start of the Tribunal, the president will ask the responsible clinician some statutory questions based on the section the patient is detained under. For example, for a patient detained under Section 3, the first question would be - *Is the person suffering from mental disorder?* If the responsible clinician answers *yes*, the president will move on to the next question. If the answer is *no*, there will be no need to go through any further questions as the person would not meet the detention criteria. These questions are to establish whether the section criteria under which the person is detained are still satisfied. If they are not, the Tribunal may discharge immediately.

Discharge criteria – Section 2

For patients appealing against their detention under Section 2, the Tribunal should discharge them if they consider that:

> the person is not suffering from mental disorder
> **or**

the mental disorder is not of a nature or degree which warrants detention in hospital for assessment or assessment followed by treatment

or

detention is not justified in the interests of the person's own health or safety or for the protection of others.

Discharge criteria – Sections 3, 37, 47 and 48

If a person is detained under Section 3, 37, 47 or 48, the Tribunal should discharge them if they consider that:

the person is not suffering from mental disorder (if the person has a learning disability that it is not associated with abnormally aggressive or seriously irresponsible conduct)

or

the mental disorder is not of a nature or degree which makes it appropriate for them to be detained in hospital for medical treatment

or

it is not necessary for the health or safety of the patient or for the protection of others that they should receive such treatment

or

appropriate treatment is not available.

(For Section 3, if the nearest relative has applied to discharge the patient and this has been barred by the responsible clinician, the third criteria above changes to: the patient, if released, would not be likely to act in a manner dangerous to themselves or others).

Discharge criteria – guardianship

If a person is under guardianship, the Tribunal can order their discharge if they consider that:

they are not suffering from mental disorder (if the person has a learning disability that it is not associated with abnormally aggressive or seriously irresponsible conduct)

or

it is not necessary in the interests of the welfare of the patient or for the protection of other persons that they should remain under such guardianship.

Discharge criteria – community treatment order

If a person is under a community treatment order, the Tribunal can order their discharge if they consider that:

they are not suffering from mental disorder

or

the mental disorder is not of a nature or degree which makes it appropriate for them to receive medical treatment

or

it is not necessary for their health or safety or for the protection of other persons that they should receive such treatment

or

it is not necessary that the responsible clinician should be able to recall them to hospital

or

appropriate medical treatment is not available.

Discharge criteria – forensic restricted sections

Under Section 73, the Tribunal should order the absolute discharge of a restricted patient where they are satisfied that:

the patient is not suffering from mental disorder (if the person has a learning disability that it is not associated with abnormally aggressive or seriously irresponsible conduct) of a nature or degree which makes it appropriate for them to be detained in hospital for medical treatment

or

it is not necessary for the health or safety of the patient or for the protection of others that they should receive such treatment

or

appropriate medical treatment is not available

and

it is not appropriate for the patient to remain liable to be recalled to hospital for further treatment.

If a patient is *absolutely* discharged they are no longer liable to be detained under the hospital order which had applied to them and the restriction order they were subject to will also no longer apply.

The Tribunal should *conditionally* discharge restricted patients where the criteria are satisfied but they consider that the patient should still be liable to be recalled (Section 41 only, see page 69). The patient must comply with the conditions of the discharge set by the Tribunal or the Ministry of Justice while conditionally discharged. The Ministry of Justice has the power to vary the conditions imposed.

The Tribunal also has the power to defer a direction for conditional discharge until such arrangements, as appear necessary to them, for the discharge have been met (for example, appropriate housing in the community).

Additional factors – Sections 47/49 and 48/49

In the case of patients under Sections 47/49 and 48/49 the Tribunal, upon an appeal being made, should notify the Ministry of Justice whether the patient is entitled to be absolutely or conditionally discharged. Further, they may propose that if the patient cannot be conditionally discharged contrary to the Tribunal's recommendation, then their detention continues in hospital.

Where the Tribunal recommends discharge, the Ministry of Justice has 90 days to notify the Tribunal whether the patient may be discharged in accordance with their recommendation. In the absence of such notice by the Ministry of Justice or an alternative direction by the Tribunal, the hospital should transfer the patient to a prison or other institution in which they might have been detained if they had not been removed to hospital under the Act. The patient will then be dealt with there as if they had not been removed.

Additional factors – Sections 47 and 48

Where a Section 47 patient is still liable to serve their sentence following discharge by a Tribunal, the Tribunal must inform the Ministry of Justice of the discharge and may also recommend that the patient stay in hospital instead of returning to prison. Alternatively the Ministry of Justice may agree to a sentenced prisoner's discharge, in which case the patient will not have to be returned to prison.

In the case of patients detained under Section 48, where the Tribunal notifies the Ministry of Justice that the patient would be entitled to absolute or conditional discharge, in the absence of a recommendation by the Tribunal, the Ministry of Justice shall direct that the patient be sent to a prison or other institution in which they might have been detained, if they had not been removed to hospital. The patient will then be dealt with as if they had not been removed.

Recommendations

Even if the Tribunal does not order discharge, they may make recommendations with a view to encouraging or facilitating a patient's future discharge. They may make any of the following recommendations:

- ➤ leave of absence
- ➤ transfer to another hospital
- ➤ transfer into guardianship
- ➤ discharge via a community treatment order
- ➤ that the patient's case be considered further in the event of any of their recommendations not being followed

General powers

The Tribunal has the following general powers:

- ✓ the power to obtain any information they consider necessary
- ✓ the power to summon witnesses
- ✓ the medical member has the power (and is required) to examine the patient

Any other doctor authorised by the patient may also examine the patient in private and inspect records relating to their detention or treatment in hospital.

Case Law

Re-detention of patients after discharge by the Tribunal

The case concerned a patient who had been granted deferred (delayed) discharge from Section 2 by a Tribunal but was then detained again under Section 3 the day before the discharge was due to take effect. At the House of Lords the judge, Lord Bingham, came to the following conclusions and declared that the detention under Section 3 was valid:

- A Tribunal can only decide upon the patient's condition at the time of the hearing and consider the foreseeable consequences of discharge.
- The Tribunal cannot make an assessment guaranteed to be accurate indefinitely or for any pre-determined period of time.
- A psychiatrist who has an opinion should not oppose or suppress that opinion because it does not comply with that of the Tribunal.
- An approved social worker [now approved mental health professional] should not apply for the detention of a patient who has been discharged by the Tribunal '...unless the approved social worker forms the reasonable and *bona fide* opinion that they have information not known to the Tribunal which puts a significantly different complexion on the case as compared with that which was before the Tribunal'.

(From the case of: R V East London and the City Mental Health Trust and another, ex parte von Brandenburg [2-3] UKHL 58. November 2003)

Code of Practice

The Tribunal can organise free interpretation services for patients. This extends beyond language and can include palantypists, signers and lip speakers.

Mental Health Act 2007

The 2007 Act made a number of changes to the automatic referral system for Tribunals. This reduced the time periods concerned so that many automatic referrals take place earlier than before (see page 96).

The term 'Hospital Managers' as used in the Act, refers to the NHS Trust (or other body such as a private hospital or care home) which detains a person. The legislation gives the Hospital Managers a number of duties and powers, the most prominent of which is the authority to discharge detained patients via Hospital Managers' hearings. This power and others can be delegated to a committee consisting of people appointed to act as managers but who are not employees of the NHS Trust. They are therefore able to make independent decisions.

Independent hospitals should ensure that those on the Hospital Managers' panel are not people that work at the hospital or have a financial interest in it.

A Hospital Managers' hearing is very similar in procedure to a Mental Health Review Tribunal (see previous chapter). However, in contrast to the Tribunal there is no requirement for the panel to contain legally or medically qualified members. The Hospital Managers' panel should contain at least three members who have appropriate experience and training.

Hospital Managers' hearings *may* take place:

- ✓ at any time at the Hospital Managers' discretion.

Hearings *must* take place:

- ✓ when a responsible clinician submits a report renewing a patient's section (including community treatment orders), even if the patient does not object to the renewal.

Hearings *must be considered:*

- ✓ when the patient requests one
  or
- ✓ if the responsible clinician under Section 25(1) submits a report stopping a nearest relative's application to discharge the patient.

In the last two situations, when deciding whether to consider the case, Hospital Managers' panels are entitled to take into account whether the Tribunal has recently considered the patient's case or is due to do so in the near future.

Limitations of Hospital Managers

The members of the panel are not in a position to make their own clinical judgments (as they do not have a medical member) and consequently, in the event of a difference of opinion, they should consider adjourning the matter in order to seek further medical or other professional advice.

Hospital Managers are not able to discharge patients under Sections 35, 36 or 38. Further, they cannot discharge restricted patients without the agreement of the Secretary of State.

Discharge criteria

The legal criteria applied by the Hospital Managers are not stated in the Act but essentially will mirror that of the Mental Health Review Tribunal. Please see previous chapter.

The Code of Practice notes that '*In all cases, hospital managers have discretion to discharge patients even if the criteria for continued detention or SCT* [community treatment order] *are met.*'

Duties

The NHS Trust or hospital authority has the ultimate obligation to ensure the proper exercise of the Hospital Managers' powers of review. In the case of care homes, the person or persons registered as owners hold that obligation.

Hospital Managers must satisfy general legal requirements when conducting their reviews. That is, the Managers must adopt and apply a procedure which is fair and reasonable, not make irrational decisions and not act unlawfully.

The Code asserts a patient's right to be informed of their right to discharge by the Hospital Managers and the distinction between this and a Tribunal hearing.

Code of Practice

The patient should be allowed to have a relative, friend or advocate attend the hearing in order to support them. Unless it is considered unsafe, the patient should always be offered the opportunity to speak to the panel alone.

Case Law

The courts have ruled that in a decision to discharge a person from section, the members of a Hospital Managers' hearing panel must all agree.

(From the case of: R (On the application of Fredrick Tagoe-Thompson) v Hospital Managers of Park Royal centre sub nov Central and North West London Mental Heath NHS Trust (2003) EWCA Civ 330)

REPORTS FOR HEARINGS

Many professionals will be required to write a report at some point for use in Mental Health Act hearings. Most commonly, social workers or community workers and responsible clinicians write reports on patients in advance of hearings. Nurses may also write reports although these are generally less formal in nature.

The Mental Health Review Tribunal has produced guidance for professionals writing reports. An outline of that guidance is given below. It lists relevant information that should be included in each report. However, for further information see *www.tribunals.gov.uk*

Social circumstances reports

- ✓ the patient's home and family circumstances

- ✓ views of the patient's nearest relative (the patient's wishes must always be ascertained prior to a consideration of whether the nearest relative needs to be consulted)

- ✓ the views of any person who plays a substantial part in the care of the patient but is not professionally concerned with it

- ✓ the views of the patient, including their concerns, hopes and beliefs in relation to the Tribunal

- ✓ the continuing opportunities for employment, or for occupation and the housing facilities available to the patient

- ✓ the effectiveness of the community support that is currently available to the patient and would continue to be available to the patient if discharged from hospital

- ✓ the patient's financial circumstances (including any entitlement to benefits)

- ✓ an assessment of the patient's strengths and any other positive factors that the Tribunal should be aware of in coming to a balanced view on whether that patient should be discharged

- ✓ a risk assessment

Medical reports

- ✓ full details of the patient's mental state, behaviour and treatment

- ✓ the relevant medical history

- ✓ whether there have ever been incidences of self-neglect or self-harm

- ✓ whether the patient has ever harmed other persons or threatened them with harm, when they were mentally disordered, together with details of any neglect, harm or threats of harm

- ✓ an assessment of the extent to which the patient or other persons would be likely to be at risk if the patient is discharged by the Tribunal, and how any such risks could best be managed

- ✓ an assessment of the patient's strengths and any other positive factors that the Tribunal should be aware of in coming to a balanced view on whether they should be discharged

- ✓ if appropriate, the reasons why the patient might be treated in the community without continued detention in hospital, but needs to remain subject to recall on a community treatment order

- ✓ details of any specific conditions concerning where the patient shall reside, whether or where they must make themselves available for examination, whether they will continue to receive medical treatment and if so where they must make themselves available for such treatment, and whether they must agree to refrain from any particular conduct if discharged

In addition to the above list, there are further considerations in relation to restricted patients.

Nursing reports

- ✓ the patient's compliance with treatment

- ✓ the level of observation to which the patient is subject

- ✓ any occasions on which the patient has been secluded or restrained, including the reasons why seclusion or restraint was considered to be necessary

- ✓ any occasions on which the patient has been absent without leave (including occasions when they failed to return when required after being granted leave of absence)

- ✓ any incidents where the patient has harmed themselves or others, or has threatened other people with violence

- ✓ a copy of the patient's current nursing plan

Information not to be disclosed to the patient

A responsible clinician, social worker, nurse or other person producing a report for a hearing may request that certain information is not disclosed to the patient. This should be written as a separate report to the main one. However, it is for the Hospital Managers or the Tribunal to decide if the information is disclosed based on whether it will cause serious harm to the physical or mental health of the patient or others.

Even if a request to withhold part of the report is granted, reports will still be disclosed in full to the patient's solicitor or legal representative as long as they agree not to show them to the patient.

Sources and earlier reports

If information has come from a source other than personal experience, this source should be disclosed. If an earlier report is referred to, this report should also be attached.

Code of Practice

It is important that the responsible clinician attends the hearing and where possible, stays for the full hearing so that they can hear all the evidence.

The author of each report or the person that will be giving evidence on their behalf in the hearing should ensure they are familiar with the contents of the report.

Where the patient is under 18 and their responsible clinician is not a child and adolescent mental health service (CAMHS) specialist, the hospital should ensure a report is prepared by a CAMHS specialist for the purpose of the hearing.

Hospitals and care homes have a legal duty both to provide information (orally and in writing) to detained patients on their rights and also to take steps to ensure they understand those rights (Sections 132 and 133). This information includes:

- details of the section under which they are detained

- the powers of that section

- the patient's rights of appeal against that section including the right to legal representation or to represent themselves

- the right to an independent mental health advocate (IMHA)

There is a statutory duty to ensure the above is done as soon as practicable after detention. The Code of Practice advises that staff giving the information should be as helpful as possible and if it appears that the patient does not understand something, they should try and explain it further using communication aids where necessary.

Additional information

There is also a duty to ensure that patients understand the following provisions of the Act and how they apply to them:

- the ways they can be discharged from section
- restrictions on discharge by the nearest relative
- consent to treatment rules
- appeals to the Mental Health Review Tribunal/Panel
- the Code of Practice
- the role of the Mental Health Act Commission/Care Quality Commission
- correspondence of patients

The nearest relative

The hospital must take practical steps (unless the patient requests otherwise) to give the nearest relative the same information as given to the patient. This should be done either when the patient is given the information or within a reasonable time afterwards.

Discharge

The person must be informed if they are discharged from detention or if the authority to detain them expires.

Unless the nearest relative has exercised their own powers of discharge (see page 116) the hospital must inform the nearest relative of a patient's impending discharge. If practical, this information should be given at least seven days before the date of discharge. This duty is negated if either the patient or the nearest relative has stated that information regarding the patient's discharge should not be given to them.

Free legal representation

The patient should also be informed of the availability of free legal assistance for Mental Health Review Tribunal appeals.

The Act makes provision for the transfer of detained patients between different hospitals, across borders within the UK and outside of the UK. The rules relating to transfers differ based on the section a person is subject to. If a person is transferred the power and responsibility to detain them is transferred to the new hospital.

Who can be transferred?

- People on short-term sections such as Sections 4 and 5(2) should not be transferred.

- People on Section 135(1) or 136 can be transferred to other places of safety during the 72 hour assessment period.

- People on longer term sections such as Sections 2, 3 and 37 can be transferred by the hospital detaining them.

- People on guardianship and community treatment orders can be transferred to other areas. For community treatment orders, the responsibility for the person can be transferred to another hospital (NHS Trust or other body) and for guardianship a new guardian can be appointed.

- People on court remand orders such as Sections 35, 36 and 38 would require permission from the court that made the order prior to transfer.

- People on forensic restricted sections such as Sections 37/41, 47/49 and 48/49 require the consent of the Ministry of Justice in order to transfer them.

Transfers between places of safety (Sections 135(1) and 136)

During the 72 hour assessment period, a person can be transferred to one or more places of safety. This transfer can be carried out by either a police officer, approved mental health professional or anyone authorised by these two. The Code of Practice states that unless it is an emergency, such a transfer should not take place without the agreement of an approved mental health professional, doctor or other healthcare professional competent to assess the risk of the move.

Transfers within a NHS Trust

The transfer of a person between different hospitals of the same NHS Trust is not classed as a transfer under the Act and so does not require any special procedures or paperwork. However, it should be noted that for court remand orders (Sections 35, 36 and 38) or restricted sections (Sections 37/41, 47/49 and 48/49) such moves should not be made without the prior permission of the court or the Ministry of Justice respectively.

Note: Some restricted sections are made out to a specific named ward or unit and any movement of that person, even to another ward within the same building, would require the prior permission of the Ministry of Justice. If a restricted section does not name a specific ward or unit and the person is going to be moved to another ward in the same building with a lower level of security, permission from the Ministry of Justice is required.

Transfers within England and Wales

Detained patients transferring to different NHS Trusts within England and Wales require Form H4 to be completed by the sending hospital (together with the original section papers). These papers should go with the transferring patient and upon arrival the receiving hospital should complete the final part of the form which authorises them to detain the patient.

Transfers within UK borders

Transfers to Scotland, Northern Ireland, the Channel Islands or the Isle of Man require the additional intervention of either the Department of Health (for Section 2, 3 or 37) or the Ministry of Justice (for restricted sections). If they agree to the transfer they can authorise the continuous detention of the person across the English or Welsh border and allow for the conversion of the relevant section to the equivalent legislation in the receiving country.

If a person is being transferred into England from another part of the UK, the same process would apply. For example, the Scottish Department of Health would issue the authority, and on admission to hospital in England the receiving hospital would complete a Form M1 or CTO9 (for community treatment orders).

Transfers outside the UK

The Act also provides the power to transfer a detained patient to countries outside the UK. This is used primarily to repatriate patients who do not have the right to live or remain in the UK. The power authorises the legal transfer of the patient (for example, in an aeroplane) to the receiving country. Once in the receiving country, it becomes that country's responsibility to apply their own legislation.

All such transfers require the prior consent of a Mental Health Review Tribunal hearing as well as authorisation by the Department of Health or the Ministry of Justice, depending on the section concerned.

Code of Practice

The Code states that the following factors should be considered in making transfer decisions:

- whether the transfer would give the patient greater access to family or friends
- the effect the transfer would have on the patient's recovery
- the availability of beds at the prospective hospital
- whether the transfer would provide the patient with an environment suitable to their cultural needs

Patients should always be involved in any decision to transfer.

The Code accepts that in some instances, the transfer may be unavoidable where the hospital can no longer offer the patient the care they need.

Contact

Mental Health Programme
Department of Health, Wellington House, 133-155 Waterloo Road, London SE1 8UG
Tel: 020 7972 4548   Fax: 020 7972 4147

Mental Health Unit
The Ministry of Justice, 2nd Floor, Fry Building, 2 Marsham Street, London SW1P 4DF
Tel: 020 7035 1484   Fax: 020 7035 8974

Further information

The Mental Health Act Commission/Care Quality Commission has produced a guidance note on the transfer of detained patients. For details visit *www.mhac.org.uk*

Mental Health Act 2007

The 2007 Act introduced new rules and guidance on the transfer of detained patients across borders to and from Scotland, Northern Ireland, Channel Islands and the Isle of Man. It also allowed for the transfer of people between places of safety under Section 135(1) and 136.

Section 117 of the Act provides a legal right to after-care services for anyone who has ever been detained under the following sections of the legislation:

Sections 3, 37, 45A, 47 and 48

Once triggered, the right to after-care is ongoing and remains in place regardless of the person's circumstances. It only ends when both health and social services jointly agree that the person no longer requires after-care. However, they cannot arrive at this conclusion whilst a person remains subject to a community treatment order.

Responsibilities

Before a responsible clinician discharges a patient or grants them leave they should ensure that:

- ✓ the patient's health and social care needs have been assessed
- ✓ those needs have been incorporated into their care plan
- ✓ the risks to the patient or others has been assessed
- ✓ if the patient is also an offender, the victim and their family have been considered

For those being discharged, the responsible clinician should also consider whether the patient meets the criteria for a community treatment order or guardianship.

Mental Health Review Tribunals and Hospital Managers' hearings

The Code of Practice advises that planning for after-care should be completed prior to a Mental Health Review Tribunal or Hospital Managers' hearing taking place in particular where there is a strong possibility of the patient being discharged.

The Care Programme Approach (CPA)

Section 117 of the Act contains the legal right to after-care, however it is through the CPA process that such after-care is assessed and delivered.

A patient's CPA should include:

- ➤ an assessment of their health and social care needs
- ➤ a care plan to provide for those needs
- ➤ a care co-ordinator to liaise with the patient and monitor their care
- ➤ regular review of the care plan with changes made where necessary

Assessment of after-care

The Code of Practice states:

'After-care is a vital component in patients' overall treatment and care. As well as meeting their immediate needs for health and social care, after-care should aim to support them in regaining or enhancing their skills, or learning new skills, in order to cope with life outside hospital.'

In order to produce a comprehensive after-care plan, the Code suggests that the following areas should be assessed in order to identify any needs or assistance the patient might need:

- continuing mental healthcare, whether in the community or on an out-patient basis
- the psychological needs of the patient and, where appropriate, of their family and carers
- physical healthcare
- daytime activities or employment

- appropriate accommodation
- identified risks and safety issues
- any specific needs arising from co-existing physical disability, sensory impairment, learning disability or autistic spectrum disorder (if relevant)
- any specific needs arising from drug, alcohol or substance misuse (if relevant)
- any parenting or caring needs
- social, cultural or spiritual needs
- counselling and personal support
- assistance in welfare rights and managing finances
- the involvement of authorities and agencies in a different area, if the patient is not going to live locally
- the involvement of other agencies, for example the probation service or voluntary organisations
- for a restricted patient, the conditions which the Secretary of State for Justice or the Tribunal has imposed or is likely to impose on their conditional discharge
- contingency plans (should the patient's mental health deteriorate) and crisis contact details

The professionals concerned should, in discussion with the patient, establish an agreed outline of the patient's needs and agree a timescale for the implementation of the various aspects of the after-care plan.

After the plan is agreed, any proposed changes should be discussed with those involved in the care plan before they are implemented. The care co-ordinator is responsible for arranging regular reviews of the care plan.

Case Law

The courts have ruled that a local authority has a mandatory duty to provide after-care under Section 117 and this after-care should not be subject to means testing. However, in providing after-care, the patient's financial position may be taken into account to establish their actual needs. For example, someone who already owned a house would not be prejudiced if social services did not provide them with housing. The courts also accept that funds are limited and services have to do the best they can with the resources available.

(From the case of: Tinsey (by his receiver and litigation friend Martin Conroy) v Sarker [2005] EWHC 192 (QB), February 2005)

Code of Practice

After-care services can include services provided by the primary care trust, local authority and other services commissioned by them. A patient is not obliged to accept after-care although this does not necessarily mean they do not need after-care services and they may later change their minds.

After-care should be regularly reviewed and should not cease just because the patient is deprived of their liberty under the Mental Capacity Act 2005 or is no longer subject to a community treatment order or has been granted leave in the community.

Further information

Department of Health (2008) *Refocusing the Care Programme Approach, Policy and Positive Practice Guidance* – download from:

www.dh.gov.uk/en/Publicationsandstatistics/Publications/PublicationsPolicyAndGuidance/ DH_083647

MENTAL HEALTH ACT COMMISSION / CARE QUALITY COMMISSION

The Mental Health Act Commission is the statutory body created by the Act to monitor the care and treatment of detained patients and the wider operation of the legislation. It is made up of members (Commissioners) with experience and knowledge of the Act. They include legal professionals, medical professionals, nurses, social workers and lay members. The Commission works under the direction of the Secretary of State for Health, however it operates as an independent statutory body.

For the year ending March 2008, Commissioners visited over 1,900 wards with detained patients and spoke to over 5,600 patients individually [7].

The Mental Health Act Commission (together with the Healthcare Commission and Commission for Social Care Inspection) will be replaced by the Care Quality Commission from April 2009.

Contact

Mental Health Act Commission
Maid Marion House, 56 Hounds Gate, Nottingham NG1 6BG

Tel: 0115 943 7100   Fax: 0115 943 7101   Website: www.mhac.org.uk

(The contact details above are expected to change from April 2009)

Functions

The Commission performs the following functions:

- ➢ Appoints registered medical practitioners as second opinion appointed doctors (SOADs) for the consent to treatment rules under the Act.

- ➢ Reviews the care and treatment of detained patients and those on community treatment orders. In order to do this, the Commission, or a person authorised by them, may at any reasonable time:
  - visit and interview a patient
  - examine a patient in private (if they are a second opinion appointed doctor)
  - ask to see a patient's records

- ➢ Review decisions to withhold post (Section 134) and may decide that the patient's post should not be withheld. The Commission's decision will be binding upon the hospital.

- ➢ Gives guidance on the practice and administration of the Act. A list of Commission guidance notes is given on page 148.

- ➢ Produces proposals for updating the Code of Practice.

General protection of detained patients

The Commission carries out the following functions for the Secretary of State for Health as detailed in Section 120 of the Act in relation to detained patients. These include:

- → **Reviewing** the use of the powers under the Act in relation to detained patients.

- → **Monitoring** the operation of the consent to treatment provisions.

- → **Visiting** and interviewing detained patients and people subject to community treatment orders or guardianship.

- → **Investigating** complaints by patients who are, or have been, detained under the Act (in relation to those periods of detention). In particular complaints that a patient believes were not dealt with satisfactorily by the hospital or NHS Trust (see below).

→ **Investigating** complaints made by Members of Parliament (MPs) regarding a detained patient. The Commission must inform the MP of the findings of any such investigation.

→ **Reporting** on its activities for the Secretary of State for Health by producing biennial reports which are presented to Parliament. The most recent report covers the period 2005 – 2007 and is entitled *Risk, Rights, Recovery* (download from *www.mhac.org.uk*).

Investigation of complaints

Any person detained under the Act has the right to complain to the Commission about the period in which they were detained. The Commission may arrange to visit and interview the patient or they may ask the hospital to use the normal NHS complaints procedure and keep the Commission informed. Complaints can also be made by a patient's relative, friend or other person, providing it refers to a particular period of detention.

The Act excludes certain matters from investigation and does not bind an investigator of a complaint to continue where they do not feel it is appropriate to do so. For example, the Commission may consider it more appropriate for the complaint to be investigated by an alternative body such as the Parliamentary and Health Service Ombudsman.

Commission visits

The Commission undertakes regular visits to hospitals, care homes, high security hospitals and any other unit that accommodates people detained under the Act. Visiting commissioners may give notice of their visit, however they are not under any obligation to do so and may visit without giving prior notice. It is an offence to refuse a commissioner access to patients or their records.

Death of detained patients

The Commission should be informed of the death of any patient detained under the Act. They will request full details of the circumstances and may send a commissioner to an inquest or other review.

Limitations

The Commission has no power to discharge a patient and can only visit and investigate issues relating to detained patients.

A Code of Practice[8] to the Act offers practical guidance on the application of the legislation. It can be downloaded from:

www.dh.gov.uk/en/Publicationsandstatistics/Publications/PublicationsPolicyAndGuidance/ DH_084597

There are separate Codes of Practice for England and Wales. The text used in this book comes from the English version.

In addition to the Code, the Department of Health has produced the *Reference Guide to the Mental Health Act* which contains other information on using the legislation (download from *www.dh.gov.uk/en/Publicationsandstatistics/index.htm*).

Legal status

The Act places a duty on staff to *'have regard'* to the guidance given in the Code of Practice. The Code itself states:

'The Code provides guidance to registered medical practitioners ("doctors"), approved clinicians, managers and staff of hospitals, and approved mental health professionals on how they should proceed when undertaking duties under the Act.

While the Act does not impose a legal duty to comply with the Code, the people listed above to whom the Code is addressed must have regard to the Code. The reasons for any departure should be recorded. Departures from the Code could give rise to legal challenge, and a court, in reviewing any departure from the Code, will scrutinise the reasons for the departure to ensure that there is sufficiently convincing justification in the circumstances.'

The Code however is not legislation but guidance and a court judgment in 2005 confirmed the position of the Code of Practice as subservient to law. The case involved a complaint that Ashworth high security hospital was implementing seclusion procedures that did not follow the requirements of the Code of Practice. The court decided that Ashworth could take such action even though it departed from the Code's guidance, as it showed clear and cogent reasons for doing so. Consequently, hospitals may depart from the Code (though not the Act itself) and develop their own practices as long as they do not breach any rights under the European Convention on Human Rights. However, there should be 'cogent' reasons for any such departure from the Code's guidance.

(From the case of: R v Ashworth Hospital Authority (Mersey Care NHS Trust) ex parte Munjaz [2005] UKHL 58)

Guiding principles

The Code of Practice begins by setting out five guiding principles. These should be considered when making decisions about a course of action under the Act. The principles work together to form a balanced set of considerations which should inform every decision. The principles are reproduced at the beginning of this book (see page 4).

The Mental Health Act 2007

The 2007 Act introduced the following changes:

- Staff have a legal duty to *'have regard'* to the Code (Section 118)
- A requirement on the Secretary of State to include a series of principles within the Code that should inform decisions made under the Act
- A new updated Code of Practice published August 2008
- The Reference Guide to the Act replaced the previous Memorandum to the Act

The Act gives specific legal powers to a detained patient's nearest relative. A nearest relative is not chosen or appointed by the patient, instead it is dictated by the legislation. The term *nearest relative* should not be confused with the term *next of kin*.

Hierarchy

The position of nearest relative is chosen in accordance with the hierarchy set out in Section 26 of the Act:

➢ **Husband or wife or civil partner**
This includes people who have lived together as husband and wife or civil partners for at least six months, as long as they are not married to someone else. If they are permanently separated, or one has deserted the other, they are excluded.

➢ **Son or daughter**
The Act also gives the outdated explanation that an 'illegitimate child' will be treated as a legitimate child of their mother. Such a child will also be the legitimate child of their father if the father has parental responsibility for them within the meaning of the Children Act.

➢ **Father or mother**

➢ **Brother or sister**
The Act does not distinguish between half and full-blood relations so, a half-sister can be treated as a sister for the purposes of this section. However, a full-blood sister will take precedence over a half-sister.

➢ **Grandparent**

➢ **Grandchild**

➢ **Uncle or aunt**

➢ **Nephew or niece**

For all of the above, if there is more than one person of equal standing in a category (ie two full-blood sisters) the eldest one will be classed as the nearest relative.

Carers

If the patient was living with, and/or cared for by, any one of the relatives in the list above, that relative will be preferred as the nearest relative regardless of their position in the hierarchy. If there are two such relatives, the hierarchy will again take effect to decide which one of them will assume the position of nearest relative.

Exclusions

Patients under the forensic Sections 35, 36, 38 or restricted patients will not be appointed a nearest relative.

Excluded relatives

The following people are excluded from being a nearest relative regardless of their position in the hierarchy:

• A non-resident of the UK, Channel Islands or the Isle of Man
• Anyone under 18 unless they are the husband/wife/civil partner Anyone with an (un-rescinded) order under Section 38 of the Sexual Offences Act 1956 which removes the relative's authority over the patient

Detained patients who are not UK residents

Normally, if a relative is not resident in the UK they are excluded by the Act. However, if the patient is not a UK resident themselves (for example, a tourist or recent migrant) then the nearest relative may be a person not resident in the UK.

Unrelated nearest relative

A person who is unrelated to the patient may also be classed as the nearest relative if they have lived with the patient for at least five years (but not as husband or wife). However, this person will be considered last in the hierarchy.

Nearest relative of a minor under guardianship

If a minor (someone under 18) is under guardianship or in the custody of a person, their nearest relative will be that person (to the exclusions of others) and not the relevant person in the hierarchy above.

Displacing (removing) a nearest relative

The patient, any relative, a person who the patient usually resides with or an approved mental health professional may apply to a County Court to have another person appointed as the nearest relative on one of the following grounds:

- the patient has no nearest relative within the meaning of the Act or it is not reasonably practicable to find out if they have such a relative or who they are.

- the nearest relative is unable to act due to mental disorder or illness.

- the nearest relative unreasonably objects to an application for Section 3 or guardianship.

- the nearest relative has exercised their power (or is likely to do so) to discharge the person without due regard to the person's welfare or the public interest.

- the nearest relative of the patient is *not a suitable person to act as such*.

The Code of Practice states that approved mental health professionals should consider applying to court to displace a nearest relative if: *'they have good reason to think that a patient considers their nearest relative unsuitable and would like them to be replaced; and it would not be reasonable in the circumstances to expect the patient, or anyone else, to make an application'*.

Delegating authority of nearest relative

A nearest relative may authorise another person to perform their functions under the Act. The following rules apply in these circumstances:

- ➢ the authorised person does not have to be related to the person
- ➢ authorisation can be given at any time
- ➢ authorisation may be revoked at any time
- ➢ authorisation lapses on the death of the nearest relative giving it

While in force, such authorisation confers the functions of the nearest relative on the person authorised, to the exclusion of the person initially defined as nearest relative. The nearest relative should put their wishes in writing and the person nominated should confirm their acceptance in writing.

Rights

The nearest relative has the right to appeal to the Mental Health Review Tribunal in the following circumstances:

- if their request to discharge the patient from Section 3 or a community treatment order has been barred by the responsible clinician

- for the same periods as the patient if they are on a community treatment order after being under Section 37, 47 or 48 before

- once every 12 months if the patient is under guardianship

- when the patient's Section 37, 47 or 48 is renewed or during the renewal period

- if they are displaced by a court from acting as nearest relative

The nearest relative also has the right to:

- receive information about the patient's treatment (unless the patient objects)

- be consulted by and challenge decisions made by an approved mental health professional to use certain detention sections

- attend a Mental Health Review Tribunal or Hospital Managers' hearing

- be informed of the patient's discharge

- be informed if the patient is transferred to another hospital

- request the local authority to assess their own needs if they provide a substantial amount of care under the Carers (Recognition and Services) Act 1995.

Powers

The nearest relative has the power to:

- delegate their powers to another person by putting this in writing

- request the discharge of the patient if under Section 2, 3, guardianship or a community treatment order

- stop an application by an approved mental health professional for detention under Section 3 or guardianship. A court would then be required to displace the relative in order to continue with the proposed detention

- authorise a doctor to visit and examine the patient in order to advise on a decision to discharge the patient

- apply for their relative to be detained under Section 2, 3 or 4 of the Act

Power to discharge

One of the most significant powers given to nearest relatives is the power to discharge a patient detained under Section 2, 3 or community treatment order. To use this power, they must inform the hospital in writing at least 72 hours before the intended discharge.

The exercise of this power is limited because it can be blocked by the responsible clinician if they believe that the patient, if discharged, is likely to act in a manner dangerous to themselves or others. This is done by the responsible clinician completing Form M2 before the end of the 72 hour notice period required for such discharge.

The nearest relative also has the power to discharge a person from guardianship. In this case, the responsible clinician has no power to prevent the discharge. However, an application to displace the nearest relative could still be made.

Appeal against a responsible clinician's objection

If discharge is blocked, the nearest relative may not exercise their powers of discharge for a further six months from the date of the responsible clinician's Form M2. However, the nearest relative may appeal against the responsible clinician's veto to discharge by applying to the Mental Health Review Tribunal within 28 days. This only applies if the patient is detained under Section 3 or a community treatment order.

Social services and the nearest relative

Approved mental health professionals have a number of duties with regard to nearest relatives:

> Before an application under Section 2 is made, or within a reasonable time thereafter, the approved mental health professional must inform the nearest relative of the patient's detention and the nearest relative's power to discharge the patient.

> Before an application under Section 3 is made, the approved mental health professional must consult the nearest relative unless such consultation is not reasonably practicable or would involve unreasonable delay.

> If the nearest relative objects to a Section 3 or guardianship application by an approved mental health professional, it cannot go ahead. However, the nearest relative may be displaced by a County Court where the objection is considered unreasonable.

> To make an assessment of the need for the patient's detention in hospital if requested to do so by their nearest relative.

The approved mental health professional should tell the patient about their right to appoint a nearest relative if they discover that the patient has no relative.

Duty to consult nearest relatives – Section 2 and 3

The Code of Practice gives circumstances in which the nearest relative need not be informed or consulted by an approved mental health professional for a Section 2 or 3 application:

- It is not practicable for the approved mental health professional to obtain sufficient information to establish the identity or location of the nearest relative, or to do so would require an excessive amount of investigation involving unreasonable delay.

- Consultation is not possible because of the nearest relative's own health or mental incapacity.

- Although physically possible, it would not be reasonably practicable to consult the nearest relative because there would be a detrimental impact on the patient which would result in the infringement of the patient's right to respect for their privacy and family life under Article 8 of the European Convention on Human Rights and which could not be justified by the benefit of the involvement of the nearest relative. Detrimental impact may include cases where patients are likely to suffer emotional distress, deterioration in their mental health, physical harm, financial or other exploitation as a result of the consultation.

Further information

The Mental Health Act Commission/Care Quality Commission has produced two guidance notes on nearest relatives (see page 148).

Mental Health Act 2007

The 2007 Act made the following changes to this part of the Act:

- Recognition of civil partners within the nearest relative hierarchy
- Patients given the right to apply to County Court to displace their nearest relative
- The addition of a new reason to displace a nearest relative because they are *'not a suitable person to act as such'*

Approved mental health professionals have a formal role within the Act and certain powers and duties placed upon them. They were introduced by the Mental Health Act 2007 and replaced the previous role of approved social workers.

Becoming an AMHP

To become an approved mental health professional, a person must meet three criteria:

1. *Professional status*

   They must be a registered social worker, first level nurse (learning disability and mental health), registered occupational therapist or chartered psychologist (with a practicing certificate from the British Psychological Society). Doctors cannot become approved mental health professionals.

2. *Training*

   They must have undertaken an approved mental health professional's course in the last five years. The course must be approved by the General Social Care Council.

3. *Competencies and approval*

   In addition to completing the training course, the Act lists a number of competencies a person must meet. Approval is granted by a local social services authority, although the person does not have to work for the local authority. Approval is given for five years at a time.

Once a person is approved they are required to complete at least 18 hours of training every year relevant to their role as an approved mental health professional. This training must be approved by the local social services authority (it does not have to be delivered or organised by the authority).

Approval to act as an approved mental health professional can be withdrawn for a number of reasons by the local authority. For example, if the person no longer meets the professional status requirement.

The role

An approved mental health professional has a number of powers and duties which include:

Assessments/applications

- ✓ making assessments for admission under Sections 2, 3 and 4
- ✓ making applications for guardianship
- ✓ making assessments of people held under Section 136
- ✓ applying for warrants to enter premises under Section 135

Nearest relative

- ✓ determining and assigning a nearest relative for Sections 2 and 3
- ✓ consulting nearest relatives when making Section 2, 3 or guardianship applications
- ✓ applying to the County Court for the appointment of an acting nearest relative and the displacement of an existing nearest relative

Working With The Mental Health Act

Absent without leave

- ✓ the power to take patients into custody and return them when they have gone absent without leave (AWOL)
- ✓ the power to take and return other patients who have absconded
- ✓ being consulted by responsible clinicians before they make reports confirming the detention of community treatment order patients who have been absent without leave for more than 28 days

Community treatment orders

- ✓ confirming that community treatment orders should be made
- ✓ approving conditions for new community treatment orders
- ✓ approving the renewal of community treatment orders
- ✓ approving the revocation of community treatment orders

Other

- ✓ requesting an independent mental health advocate for a detained patient
- ✓ the power to convey patients to hospital when an application for detention is completed
- ✓ taking or authorising another person to transfer a person under Section 135(1) or 136 to another place of safety
- ✓ the right to enter and inspect premises under Section 115

Transition

People who were approved social workers on 2nd November 2008 automatically became approved mental health professionals for the remainder of their existing period of approval (as an approved social worker) on the 3rd November 2008.

Further Information

For more information on the role of approved mental health professionals see *www.mhact.csip.org.uk*.

Statutory guidance on the role of approved mental health professionals is contained in *The Mental Health (Approved Mental Health Professionals) (Approval) (England) Regulations 2008, No. 1206.* This can be downloaded from:

www.opsi.gov.uk/si/si2008/uksi_20081206_en_1

Approved and responsible clinicians have a formal role within the Act and certain powers and duties placed upon them. They were introduced by the Mental Health Act 2007 and replaced the previous role of responsible medical officers. These titles allow a broader range of professionals to take on more formal responsibility under the Act. Of the approved clinicians involved in a patient's care, one will be given the responsibility of being a patient's 'responsible clinician' and will hold further powers.

Becoming an approved clinician

To become an approved clinician a person must meet three criteria:

1. Professional status

The role of approved clinician is limited to the following professionals:

- registered medical practitioners (doctors)
- chartered psychologists
- registered social workers
- first level nurses (mental health or learning disability)
- registered occupational therapists

2. Training

Any one of the above professionals must undertake a specific training course so they may become 'approved'.

3. Competencies and approval

In addition to completing the training course, the Act lists a number of competencies a person must meet. Approval is given by Strategic Health Authorities (SHA) (or Primary Care Trusts if delegated to do so by the SHA) and is given for five year periods.

Section 12 approved

Any doctor that becomes an approved clinician will automatically also be classed as being Section 12 approved for the purposes of the Act.

Role of approved clinician

An approved clinician has a number of powers and duties including:

- ✓ the use of the holding power under Section 5(2)
- ✓ the power to visit and examine patients under Section 24
- ✓ authority to provide evidence to courts in relation to forensic sections
- ✓ authority to provide certificates to authorise treatment under Part 4

Role of responsible clinician

The responsible clinician will be the approved clinician with overall responsibility for the patient's care and will largely adopt the role previously undertaken by the responsible medical officer. A responsible clinician has a number of specific powers and duties:

- ✓ granting leave to patients
- ✓ revoking a period of leave and recalling patients
- ✓ discharging patients from detention, guardianship or community treatment orders
- ✓ renewing a patient's section
- ✓ with the agreement of the approved mental health professional, setting conditions for a community treatment order
- ✓ varying or suspending conditions of a community treatment order

Working With The Mental Health Act

- ✓ recalling a patient from a community treatment order
- ✓ blocking a nearest relative's attempt to discharge a patient
- ✓ providing certificates to authorise treatment under Part 4 (only for treatment they can professionally prescribe)
- ✓ providing evidence to courts and the Ministry of Justice as required

The Code of Practice notes that it is necessary to allocate a responsible clinician promptly upon the patient's detention in hospital. The choice of responsible clinician should be based on the individual needs of the patient concerned. For example, where psychological therapies are central to the patient's treatment it may be appropriate for a psychologist to act as the responsible clinician.

The choice of responsible clinician should be reviewed over time because as the needs of the patient change, so too may the most appropriate responsible clinician change. If patients are transferred to different hospitals, the responsible clinician should take the lead in identifying the next responsible clinician.

Code of Practice

There may be circumstances where the responsible clinician is qualified with respect to the patient's main assessment and treatment needs but is not appropriately qualified to be in charge of a subsidiary treatment needed by the patient (eg medication which the responsible clinician is not qualified to prescribe). In such situations, the responsible clinician will maintain their overall responsibility for the patient's care, but another appropriately qualified professional will take responsibility for a specified treatment or intervention.

Where the person in charge of a particular treatment is not the patient's responsible clinician, the person in charge of the treatment should ensure that the responsible clinician is kept informed about the treatment and that treatment decisions are discussed with the responsible clinician in the context of the patient's overall care.

Transition

Section 12 doctors that acted as responsible medical officers in the 12 months ending on 2nd November 2008, automatically became approved clinicians on the 3rd November 2008. They will be approved until the end of the current Section 12 approval or for 12 months whichever is later. After this they will have to re-apply for approval but not have to undertake the initial training course for approved clinicians.

Section 12 doctors that had not acted as responsible medical officers are also classed as approved clinicians if they were in charge of the treatment for a person within the 12 months that ended on 2nd November 2008. Approval is for 12 months only and further approval will require completion of the approved clinicians' training course.

Doctors that had not acted as responsible medical officers or been in charge of a person's treatment are also approved if they were a Section 12 doctor with the post of consultant psychiatrist within the 18 months that ended on 2nd November 2009. They will be approved for 12 months and further approval will require completion of the approved clinicians training course.

Further information

For more information on the role of approved and responsible clinicians see *www.mhac.csip.org.uk*.

The statutory guidance on approved clinicians is contained in the *National Health Service Act 2006: Mental Health Act 1983 Approved Clinician (General) Directions 2008.* This can be downloaded from:

www.dh.gov.uk/en/Publicationsandstatistics/Publications/PublicationsLegislation/DH_086 548

Independent mental health advocates (IMHAs) were introduced by the Mental Health Act 2007 as a statutory right for people detained under the legislation. Their objective is to provide support to patients detained under the Act. In carrying out their role, they may be involved in providing patients with information on their rights, medication and any restrictions or conditions to which they are subject. The IMHA does not give their own personal views, but simply those of the patient they represent.

In Wales the IMHA service is due to start before the end of 2008 whilst in England it is expected to begin in April 2009.

The right to an independent mental health advocate

Detained patients

The right to an IMHA is available if the person is:

> - detained under the Act (even if they are on leave under Section 17)
> - conditionally discharged
> - under guardianship
> - community patients (subject to a community treatment order)

The Act uses the term 'qualifying patient' to describe the above group of patients who qualify for the right to the IMHA service.

The right to an IMHA is not available if the patient is subject to short-term detention under Section 4, 5(2), 5(4), 135(1) or 136:

Informal (voluntary) patients

In addition, people who are not detained under the Act also have a right to an IMHA if they are:

- being considered for treatment under Section 57 (neurosurgery for mental disorder or surgical implantation of hormones to reduce male sex drive)
- under 18 and being considered for electro-convulsive therapy (ECT) or any other treatment to which Section 58A applies (medication administered as part of ECT)

Those listed above remain eligible to have an IMHA until the treatment is finished (or stopped) or it is decided that they will not be given the treatment for the time being.

Duty to provide information about the IMHA Service

- ✓ The NHS Trust or other organisation detaining a person have a legal duty to inform them (verbally and in writing) of their rights under the Act. This includes the right to an IMHA. Standard rights leaflets are produced by the Department of Health to assist in this.

- ✓ Where a qualifying patient has a nearest relative, the NHS Trust or other organisation detaining the person must also provide a copy of the same information, in writing, to the nearest relative (unless the qualifying patient requests otherwise).

Training and independence

Independent mental health advocates must undertake a national training qualification. For details see: *www.mhact.csip.org.uk*.

IMHA services are provided by organisations independent of the NHS and local authorities, usually charities and non-profit organisations. Around England and Wales each borough, county or other region will commission a local IMHA service through local authority or Primary Care Trust commissioning arrangements.

Referrals

Anybody can make a referral to an IMHA. However, under the Act, an IMHA has a duty to *'comply with any reasonable request'* to visit and interview a qualifying person when made by any of the following people:

- nearest relative
- responsible clinician
- approved mental health professional

The referral should be discussed with the patient first. A referral would not be appropriate where it is apparent the patient does not want the services of the IMHA.

A qualifying patient may also request the support of an IMHA themselves. The patient can decide to end their contact with the IMHA service at any time.

Qualifying patients lacking capacity

If a person referred to an IMHA lacks capacity to instruct or work with the IMHA, it will be for the IMHA to decide on the support they give. There is no explicit information in the Act on this. It is suggested that an approach similar to that taken in the Mental Capacity Act would be appropriate, that is, assessing what may be in the person's best interests and for the IMHA to act accordingly.

Qualifying patients with capacity

If the person has capacity and does not wish to have the assistance of the IMHA, the IMHA will not act.

Other advocacy/legal services

The Code of Practice states: *'Independent mental health advocacy services do not replace any other advocacy and support services that are available to patients, but are intended to operate in conjunction with those services. The involvement of an IMHA does not affect a patient's right (nor the right of their nearest relative) to seek advice from a lawyer. Nor does it affect any entitlement to legal aid'.*

The role

The help an IMHA can provide to the patient (as listed by the legislation) includes help in obtaining information about and an understanding of the following areas:

Powers of the Act
- the provisions of the Act that apply to the patient (including the reasons/process of their detention)
- any conditions or restrictions which apply to them because of the Act (for example, leave of absence)

Treatment
- what and why medical treatment (if any) is being proposed or given to them
- the powers of the Act under which treatment is to be provided
- the patient's right to refuse treatment

Rights
- what rights the person has under the Act (including the rights of others, for example the nearest relative)
- any available assistance (by way of representation or otherwise) in exercising those rights

Authority/powers of an IMHA

Meeting the patient in private

When the IMHA is instructed by the patient, nearest relative, approved mental health professional or responsible clinician the IMHA has a right to meet the patient in private. Anyone who prevents them doing so without reasonable cause may be guilty of the offence of obstruction under Section 129.

The Code of Practice states *'Patients should have access to a telephone on which they can contact the independent mental health advocacy service and talk to them in private'.*

Speaking to staff treating the patient

The IMHA has the right to interview anyone concerned with the patient's medical treatment, provided it is for the purpose of assisting them in their role as an IMHA.

The Code of Practice notes *'If an IMHA speaks to a professional without the consent of the patient, it should be understood that the professional may not share confidential information with the IMHA'.*

Access to records

If the patient has capacity and consents, the IMHA can request to see:

- any records relating to their detention or treatment in hospital or a registered establishment
  and
- any records relating to their after-care services under Section 117
  and
- any records of, or held by, social services which relate to the patient.

If the patient lacks capacity concerning access to records the IMHA must ensure that:

1. viewing the records would not conflict with a decision made by an attorney or deputy or the Court of Protection and
2. the record holder believes the information is *relevant* to the help being provided by the advocate and
3. it is *appropriate*.

The Code of Practice states *'When seeking access to the records of a patient that lacks capacity, the IMHA will normally be asked to declare why access is being sought and the nature of the information being requested.'*

Code of Practice

The Code states that IMHAs should have access to wards and units on which patients are resident and be able to attend relevant meetings and ward rounds when asked to do so by the patient.

Further information

For more information on independent mental health advocacy: *www.mhact.csip.org.uk*

Sections 130A-D of the Act detail the role and function of independent mental health advocates. See: *www.publications.parliament.uk/pa/pabills/200607/mental_health.htm.*

Chapter 20 of the Code of Practice also gives guidance on advocacy.

CONFLICTS OF INTEREST

Potential conflicts of interest that may arise when decisions are taken to detain people under the Act are addressed in the *Mental Health (Conflicts of Interest) (England) Regulations 2008 No.1205*.

Download: *www.dh.gov.uk/en/Healthcare/NationalServiceFrameworks/Mentalhealth/ DH_077359#_13*

The regulations address four key areas where a conflict of interest may arise – financial, business, professional and personal relationships. Approved mental health professionals making applications for detention and doctors making recommendations to detain a patient are known as '*assessors*' in the regulations.

Financial conflict

In order to detain a patient, many sections require that two doctors provide a medical recommendation. If the hospital proposing to detain a patient is a private hospital, both medical recommendations cannot be made by doctors working at that hospital (this rule does not apply to NHS hospitals).

Approved mental health professionals making applications for detention and doctors making medical recommendations for the purposes of detaining a patient will have a conflict of interest if their fee is dependent on the conclusions of their assessment. That is, they are paid a fee only if they recommend the patient is detained.

Business conflict

An assessor should not be in business with the other assessor, patient, or the nearest relative (if the nearest relative made the application for admission or assessment).

Professional conflict

The assessor should not directly manage or employ another of the assessors, the patient or the nearest relative (if they are the applicant).

The assessor and patient should not be part of the same team. The three assessors should not all be part of the same team (for example the same Community Mental Health Team). However, this rule does not apply if, in the assessor's opinion, it is of urgent necessity for an application to be made and a delay would involve serious risk to the health or safety of the patient or others.

Personal relationships

An assessor should not have a personal relationship with any other assessor, the patient or the nearest relative (if they are the applicant).

A personal relationship exists where the assessor is either the spouse, ex-spouse, civil partner, ex-civil partner, living with the person as if they were a spouse or civil partner, parent, sister, half-sister, brother, half-brother, son, daughter, uncle, aunt, grandparent, grandchild, first cousin, nephew, niece, parent-in-law, grandparent-in-law, grandchild-in-law, sister-in-law, brother-in-law, son-in-law or daughter-in-law of another assessor or the patient or the nearest relative.

The above list includes step relationships.

Community treatment orders

The regulations do not cover people under community treatment orders or Part III of the Act (court/prison sections). However the Code of Practice suggests that similar principles should be applied by staff.

Working With The Mental Health Act

Section 127 of the Act contains a criminal offence for the ill-treatment or wilful neglect of people who have a mental disorder. It is punishable by a maximum of five years of imprisonment.

Legal criteria

- Any employee of a hospital or care home who ill-treats or wilfully neglects an in-patient or out-patient with a mental disorder on the premises of the hospital or care home.

In addition it also extends to:

- any individual who is a guardian or otherwise caring for a mentally disordered person under the Act who ill-treats or wilfully neglects the person in their care.

- any individual who ill-treats or wilfully neglects a person with mental disorder they are caring for. This can be on any premises and applies even if the person is not detained under the Act.

There is no requirement for the mental disorder to be diagnosed or for the person to have received treatment, they can simply appear to be suffering from a mental disorder.

Case Law

A single act can be enough to satisfy the criteria of this section. In this case a slap to the patient's face.

(From the case of: R v Holmes [1979] Crim. L. R. 52, Bodmin Crown Court)

Other offences

The Act also contains a number of other criminal offences:

- committing forgery (Section 126)
- making false statements (Section 126)
- assisting patients to go absent without leave (Section 128)
- obstruction (Section 129)

The Mental Capacity Act 2005

An offence of ill-treatment or wilful neglect is also contained in the Mental Capacity Act 2005 in relation to people lacking capacity.

Sexual Offences Act 2003

This legislation contains a series of offences designed to protect people with mental health problems from sexually abusive acts by others including care workers.

Mental Health Act 2007

The 2007 Act increased the maximum term of imprisonment for the offence in Section 127 (ill-treatment or wilful neglect) to five years.

VOLUNTARY (INFORMAL) PATIENTS

At any given time, approximately 57% of people on mental health wards are voluntary (informal) patients[1]. Section 131 of the Mental Health Act states that although the legislation can be used to detain and treat people against their will, it does not have to be used at all and any person can admit themselves voluntarily and stay in hospital as an informal patient.

Rights of informal patients

If a patient is in hospital informally and therefore not detained under the Act, no restrictions may be placed upon them. Informal patients have the following legal rights:

✓ They must be free to come and go as they please and without restriction.

✓ They cannot be forcibly medicated.

✓ They can discharge themselves at any time.

✓ They can agree to a care plan (or 'contract') but they are not bound by it.

Patients lacking capacity

A person must have capacity to admit themselves voluntarily to hospital. If they lack capacity to consent to hospital admission and they are not admitted using the Mental Health Act then the Mental Capacity Act 2005 must be used.

Code of Practice

'The threat of detention must not be used to induce a patient to consent to admission to hospital or to treatment (and is likely to invalidate any apparent consent).'

'Although the Act does not impose any duties to give information to informal patients, these patients should be made aware of their legal position and rights. Local policies and arrangements about movement around the hospital and its grounds must be clearly explained to the patients concerned. Failure to do so could lead to a patient mistakenly believing that they are not allowed freedom of movement, which could result in an unlawful deprivation of their liberty.'

However, if an informal patient wishes to discharge themselves against the judgment of the mental health team, they may be assessed and if they meet the criteria of the Act they could then be detained.

The Mental Capacity Act 2005 (Capacity Act) provides the legal framework to assess a person's mental capacity to make decisions for themselves in relation to finance, health and social care. It provides additional powers to make decisions on behalf of a person that lacks capacity to make such decisions themselves. Moreover, it allows those with capacity to plan ahead for their future care and treatment if they were ever to lose capacity.

Anyone aged 16 and over with an impairment or disturbance (including mental disorder) in the functioning of the mind or brain (whether temporary or long-term) comes within the scope of the Capacity Act. The impairment or disturbance does not in itself mean the person lacks capacity but that the test to assess their capacity may be applied. In many cases, this will be unnecessary. However, if staff are alerted to the possibility that the person may lack capacity, they can assess the patient. The test should only be used at the time a decision is required and only for that particular decision (health, social care or financial).

The two Acts are inextricably linked, interacting in many areas. The Code of Practice states 'It will be difficult for professionals involved in providing care for people with mental health problems to carry out their work (including their responsibilities under the [Mental Health] Act) without an understanding of key concepts in the Capacity Act.'

This chapter looks at the impact of the Capacity Act on the Mental Health Act. It does not give a full explanation of the Capacity Act. For more information on the Capacity Act itself see *Further information* at the end of this chapter (page 135).

Facts

Recent research[9] indicates that 86% of patients detained under the Mental Health Act lack capacity to make decisions in relation to their mental health treatment. The study found that the proportion of patients who lacked capacity varied depending on the diagnosis, the highest being 97% for mania down to 4% for personality disorder.

Capacity to consent or make a decision

There must be evidence of an impairment or disturbance in the functioning of the mind or brain before the test can be applied. Some examples include dementia, brain injury, mental disorder, learning disability or the symptoms of alcohol or drug misuse.

The test of capacity is designed to be time and decision specific. For example, a person may need to be assessed in relation to their capacity to consent to treatment on admission. In order to establish whether they could consent to treatment, the following four-part test would be applied in relation to the proposed treatment. Can the patient:

1. understand the information relevant to the decision (including consequences)
2. retain that information long enough to make a decision
3. use or weigh (take into account) the information
4. communicate a decision (in any form recognised by the assessor)

If the person is not able to do any one of the above, they will be assessed as lacking capacity at that time, for that particular decision.

Note: When the Mental Health Act refers to a person having *capacity* to consent, it means capacity as defined and assessed under the Capacity Act.

Admission to hospital

Before the Capacity Act came into force, admission to hospital was either as an informal (voluntary) patient or under the Mental Health Act (whether or not the person had capacity). This has now changed and because of the Capacity Act admission to hospital now has three routes:

1. Informal/voluntary – the person has capacity to consent to admission and agrees to admission.

2. Capacity Act – the person lacks capacity to consent to admission and the powers of the Capacity Act are used to admit them.

3. Mental Health Act – the person has capacity or lacks capacity and the powers of the Mental Health Act are used.

An alternative to detention under the Mental Health Act

Where previously there may have been little choice about the need to use the powers of the Mental Health Act, the introduction of the Capacity Act has changed this. If the powers of the Mental Health Act are being considered to treat a person who is over 16 and lacks capacity to consent to care or treatment, consideration must first be given to using the Capacity Act. This is because, in the majority of cases, the Capacity Act would represent a less restrictive option than using the detention powers of the Mental Health Act.

The Code of Practice gives a number of examples of this situation. The most common example is where a person is being assessed for detention under Section 2 or 3. If the person being assessed lacks capacity to consent to their admission and treatment in hospital, the Capacity Act should be considered. However, if any of the following apply, using the Mental Health Act would be more appropriate:

1. The person had an advance decision refusing treatment for mental disorder. Using the Capacity Act would mean that treatment for mental disorder could not be given as it could not override the authority of the advance decision. To override an advance decision refusing mental health treatment, detention under the Mental Health Act would become necessary.

2. The person needs to be restrained regularly or for prolonged periods or because of the risk they present to others. Although the Capacity Act contains a power of restraint, it is limited in its use. It does not allow restraint to be used to prevent harm to others or to be so extensive as to result in a deprivation of liberty. In this case, the Mental Health Act would be more appropriate. See also the note below on the Deprivation of Liberty Safeguards.

3. The person may regain their capacity and will then refuse treatment. Once a person regains capacity to consent to care or treatment, they can make their own decision. The Capacity Act can no longer be applied to provide their care or treatment.

4. The person lacks capacity in relation to some areas of the proposed mental health treatment but has capacity in other areas and will refuse that element of treatment.

5. The person needs the compulsory powers of the Mental Health Act. For example because detention allows for their continued observation and assessment in order to monitor the effects of new treatment.

Restraint

The Capacity Act contains powers to restrain people who lack capacity if it is in their best interests and they would come to harm by not being restrained, provided the restraint is a proportionate response to the likelihood and seriousness of the harm.

For example, if a patient requires restraint to stop them leaving a ward, the Capacity Act could be used rather than detention under the Mental Health Act, if the person lacked capacity and they would come to harm if not restrained. Another example would be using restraint to provide treatment to a person that lacked capacity to consent.

This power of restraint does not allow staff to detain the person.

Detention under the Capacity Act

The Capacity Act will, from April 2009, contain a power that allows for the detention of people who lack capacity. This is called the 'Deprivation of Liberty Safeguards' (DOLS) within the Capacity Act. This will provide a direct alternative to using the Mental Health Act in certain cases.

The power to detain a person under the deprivation of liberty safeguards can be applied to people in hospitals and care homes if the person is 18 or over, has a mental disorder, lacks capacity in relation to their care and treatment and would come to harm if they were not detained.

For more details on the deprivation of liberty safeguards contact: dols@dh.gsi.gov.uk.

Website:www.dh.gov.uk/en/SocialCare/Deliveringadultsocialcare/MentalCapacity/MentalCapacityActDeprivationofLibertySafeguards/index.htm

Consent to treatment

If a person has capacity to make a treatment decision, they can then either consent to that treatment or refuse it. If they refuse it, the Mental Health Act may be used to override their refusal of consent if deemed appropriate.

The Code of Practice states:

'Consent is the voluntary and continuing permission of a patient to be given a particular treatment, based on a sufficient knowledge of the purpose, nature, likely effects and risks of that treatment, including the likelihood of its success and any alternatives to it. Permission given under any unfair or undue pressure is not consent.'

'By definition, a person who lacks capacity to consent does not consent to treatment, even if they co-operate with the treatment or actively seek it.'

'Although the Mental Health Act permits some medical treatment for mental disorder to be given without consent, the patient's consent should still be sought before treatment is given, wherever practicable. The patient's consent or refusal should be recorded in their notes, as should the treating clinician's assessment of the patient's capacity to consent. All assessments of a patient's capacity should be fully recorded in their notes'.

Treatment Scenarios

There are a number of cases where the two Acts can be used together.

Physical treatments

The Mental Health Act is limited to the treatment of mental disorder. It does not extend to treatment for physical health unrelated to mental disorder. Therefore, if a person detained under Section 3 also lacked capacity to consent to treatment for their diabetes, the powers of the Mental Health Act could not provide the appropriate legal authority to give this treatment. Instead, the Capacity Act could be used to make a best interests decision, to treat the patient for their diabetes, for example, by giving insulin. Section 3 of the Mental Health Act would remain in place for treatment of their mental disorder and would be unaffected by the use of the Capacity Act in this way.

Exclusions to treatment for mental disorder

Sections 4, 5(2), 5(4), 35, 135(1), 136, guardianship and conditional discharge do not provide any power to give people treatment under the Mental Health Act. Therefore treatment for mental disorder cannot be given if the person has capacity and refuses. However, if the person lacks capacity, the Capacity Act could provide the authority to give the person treatment for their mental disorder.

Community treatment orders

The treatment rules for community treatment orders under the Mental Health Act make explicit reference to capacity and other parts of the Capacity Act. For full details see page 85.

Electro-convulsive therapy

The treatment rules for electro-convulsive therapy under the Mental Health Act make explicit reference to capacity and other parts of the Capacity Act. For full details see page 82.

A person that is not detained under the Mental Health Act and lacks capacity to consent to electro-convulsive therapy can be given this treatment using the powers of the Capacity Act. Treatment could only be given once a best interests decision had been made under the Capacity Act. Further, the person would qualify for an independent mental capacity advocate (IMCA) if there was no person appropriate to consult as part of making the best interests decision.

Advance Decisions

An advance decision (previously known as a living will) is a statement by a person with capacity stating their refusal of treatment in case they ever lack capacity with regard to that treatment in the future. It can be a verbal or written statement except but it must be in writing if the person wishes to refuse life-sustaining treatment. People can make advance decisions to refuse treatment for mental disorder as for any other treatment. An advance decision only comes into force if and when the person concerned lacks capacity and the stated treatment is being proposed.

The authority of advance decisions affects the Mental Health Act in a number of ways:

- Electro-convulsive therapy – see page 82.

- Community treatment orders – a person can have an advance decision to refuse treatment and this will have effect upon the community treatment order if the person lacks capacity. But if the treatment is classed as urgent, this will override the power of the advance decision (see page 85).

- Sections 4, 5(2), 5(4), 35, 135(1), 136, guardianship and conditional discharge – these Mental Health Act sections are not covered by any treatment powers consequently, an advance decision to refuse treatment for mental disorder will have authority and the treatment cannot be provided.

- Sections 2, 3, 37, 47, 48 – these Sections will override an advance decision under the Capacity Act. However, the Code of Practice states: '*Even where clinicians may lawfully treat a patient compulsorily under the Mental Health Act, they should, where practicable, try to comply with the patient's wishes as expressed in an advance decision. They should, for example, consider whether it is possible to use a different form of treatment not refused by the advance decision.*'

Lasting Powers of Attorney (LPA)

When a person has capacity, they can name a person(s) of their choice to become their attorney in the future, should they lack capacity to make decisions themselves (health, social care or financial). If the person does lose capacity in the future, the attorney will consent to or refuse treatment on behalf of the person (if they have authority with regard to health).

Even if a person is detained under the Mental Health Act, any personal welfare (health and social care) attorney they appointed while they had capacity can provide authority for treatment that falls outside the scope of the Mental Health Act. The detained person must lack capacity to consent to the care or treatment themselves, before the attorney's powers can be used. However the attorney's powers may have limitations, so staff will need to check the attorney's authority before providing care or treatment.

A healthcare attorney also has the right of appeal on behalf of a detained patient who lacks capacity to exercise this right.

Where a person lacking capacity is being assessed for admission under either Section 2 or 3 of the Mental Health Act, the approved mental health professional should take reasonable steps to consult with any personal welfare attorney the person has. If the person is being assessed by a second opinion appointed doctor, the doctor should also consult the attorney.

The treatment rules for electro-convulsive therapy and community treatment orders make reference to attorneys in their procedures (see pages 82 and 85).

Deputies

Deputies are similar to attorneys in that they have specific authority under the Capacity Act to make decisions on behalf of people who lack capacity. Rather than being chosen by the person prior to them losing capacity, they are appointed by the Court of Protection once a person has lost capacity. Most deputies will only deal with the financial affairs of people who lack capacity (whether detained under the Mental Health Act or not). However some deputies will also have authority to make health and/or social care decisions.

If a person is detained under the Mental Health Act, a personal welfare (health and social care) deputy will provide authority for treatment that falls outside of the Mental Health Act if the person lacks capacity to consent to this treatment themselves. However, staff should check the scope of the deputy's powers before providing any care or treatment.

A personal welfare (health and social care) deputy also has the right of appeal on behalf of a detained patient who lacks capacity to exercise this right themselves.

Where a person has a personal welfare (health and social care) deputy and they lack capacity and they are being assessed for Section 2 or 3 the approved mental health professional should take reasonable steps to consult them. If the person is being assessed by a second opinion appointed doctor the doctor should consult the deputy.

The treatment rules for electro-convulsive therapy and community treatment orders make reference to deputies in their procedures (see pages 82 and 85).

Independent mental capacity advocates (IMCA)

The Capacity Act contains a right to advocacy for some people who lack capacity when certain decisions are being made. This is a different right to advocacy from that provided within the Mental Health Act. However, people detained under the Mental Health Act may also be eligible for advocacy under the Capacity Act in certain situations.

If a person is detained under the Mental Health Act, and serious medical treatment (not for mental disorder) is being proposed and they have no one appropriate to consult in helping to determine their best interests, the NHS organisation concerned is obliged to use an independent mental capacity advocate.

In addition, if a person is detained under the Mental Health Act and they are subject to vulnerable adult procedures, the NHS or local authority (social services) have a discretionary right to request an independent mental capacity advocate.

Care programme approach (CPA)

The Code of Practice notes that in drawing up an after-care plan for a patient that lacks capacity, any personal welfare attorney or deputy they have should be involved. For any care decisions that fall outside the scope of the Mental Health Act, the consent of an attorney or deputy (with personal welfare authority) will be essential to allow the care plan to go ahead.

Further information

Working with the Mental Capacity Act 2005 (2006) Steven Richards and Aasya F Mughal ISBN: 978-0-9552349-0-3

Tel: 01256 398 928   Email: *books@matrixtrainingassociates.com*

Online: *www.matrixtrainingassociates.com or www.waterstones.com*

Further information on the Act can also be obtained from:

Office of the Public Guardian, Archway Tower, 2 Junction Road, London N19 5SZ

Tel: 0845 330 2900   Email: *customerservices@publicguardian.gsi.gov.uk*

Online: *www.publicguardian.gov.uk*

Mental Health Act 2007

The 2007 Act introduced the term 'capacity' into the Mental Health Act and specific reference to the Capacity Act in relation to treatment for electro-convulsive therapy and community treatment orders. Further, it amended the Capacity Act so that a person may be lawfully detained using the deprivation of liberty safeguards (DOLS).

Which Act to use – Mental Health Act or the Capacity Act?
There are several factors to consider when deciding which is the most appropriate Act to use at any given time. This table considers some of the key questions which need to be answered.

	YES	NO
Is the person under 16?	Only the Mental Health Act can be used.	Either the Mental Health Act or the Capacity Act can be used.
Do they have a mental disorder?	Either the Mental Health Act or the Capacity Act can be used.	The Capacity Act can be used if the person has any *'impairment or disturbance of mind or brain'*.
Is the proposed treatment for mental disorder?	Either the Mental Health Act or the Capacity Act can be used.	If the person lacks capacity, only the Capacity Act can be used.
Do they have capacity to consent to treatment?	Only the Mental Health Act can be used to treat them if they refuse treatment.	Either the Mental Health Act or the Capacity Act can be used. Note: if the person's capacity will be regained in the near future the Capacity Act will be of limited use.
Do they meet the criteria for detention under the Mental Health Act?	Either the Mental Health Act or the Capacity Act can be used (if they lack capacity).	Only the Capacity Act can be used. Note: this could include Deprivation of Liberty Safeguards under the Capacity Act.
Do they have an advance decision refusing treatment for mental disorder?	To override an advance decision the Mental Health Act would have to be used. Note: special rules apply to electro-convulsive therapy.	Either the Mental Health Act or the Capacity Act can be used.
Does their lasting power of attorney or deputy or a Court of Protection ruling refuse treatment for mental disorder?	To override this the Mental Health Act would have to be used. Note: special rules apply to electro-convulsive therapy.	Either the Mental Health Act or the Capacity Act can be used.
Is prolonged and regular restraint going to be needed?	The Mental Health Act is most appropriate for mental health hospitals BUT Deprivation of Liberty Safeguards under the Capacity Act could be used instead.	Either the Mental Health Act or the Capacity Act can be used.
Is restraint needed because of the risk of harm to others?	The Mental Health Act should be used.	Either the Mental Health Act or the Capacity Act can be used.
Could the Capacity Act be used as a less restrictive option?	Use the Capacity Act as the starting point.	Use the Mental Health Act.

In general, the Act does not have a minimum age limit except in relation to guardianship where the minimum age is 16.

If it is necessary to admit and/or treat a child or young person in hospital, the local authority (social services) and the NHS should ensure they are familiar with both the Mental Health Act and other relevant legislation which is listed at the end of this chapter.

Facts

On any one day, there are just over 300 young people under the age of 18 who are in hospital and detained under the Act across England and Wales[1].

Special rules for those under 18

The Act contains a number of special rules for young people under the age of 18. The majority of these were introduced by the Mental Health Act 2007. Some of the rules apply whether or not the young person is detained.

Admission

From 1st January 2008, a person aged 16-17 who has capacity can consent to or refuse admission to hospital as an informal (voluntary) patient and their decision cannot be overridden by those with parental responsibility (usually parents).

Suitable accommodation

Where a young person under 18 is admitted to hospital (informal or detained), the managers of that hospital must ensure that the environment in the hospital is suitable, having regard to their age, but subject to their needs. This rule is not due to come into force until April 2010. However, the Code advises hospitals to take any steps they reasonably can to comply with the duty before it is a legal requirement.

Consultation requirement

When young people under 18 are admitted to hospital (informal or detained), the managers must consult a person who appears to them to have knowledge or experience of cases involving those under 18. Typically, this will mean that a child or adolescent mental health services (CAMHS) professional will need to be involved in decisions about the patient's accommodation, care and facilities for education in the hospital. This rule is not due to come into force until April 2010.

Assessing for detention

The Code of Practice states that when a young person under 18 is being assessed for detention under the Act, at least one of the people involved in the assessment (one of the two medical practitioners or the approved mental health professional) *should* be a clinician specialising in CAMHS. Where this is not possible, a CAMHS clinician should be consulted as soon as possible.

Mental Health Review Tribunal

A person under 18, detained under the Act, must automatically be referred for a Tribunal hearing by the hospital if they have not appealed during the first six months of detention and then yearly, if they do not appeal themselves. (This rule provides additional protection for young people because the same rule applies for adults after the first six months but then, not until three years has passed).

Electro-convulsive therapy

If a person under 18 is being considered for electro-convulsive therapy (whether detained or not), they must always consent if they are able to, that is, they are Gillick competent if they are under 16 or have the mental capacity to consent if they are 16-17. Further, a second opinion appointed doctor must always be called before ECT can be given (see page 82). In emergencies these rules change (see page 84).

<u>Neurosurgery or the implantation of hormones</u>

If any treatment under Section 57 is proposed, it can only be given with the young person's consent. A person with parental responsibility cannot provide this consent where the young person cannot consent themselves.

<u>Community treatment orders</u>

The treatment of young people under 16 subject to a community treatment order is covered by special rules (see page 85).

Code of Practice

The Code of Practice sets out the following special considerations for children:

- children should be kept informed about their care and treatment
- children's views and wishes should be sought and considered
- the impact of their wishes on their parents (or those with parental responsibility) should also be considered
- intervention due to mental disorder should be the least restrictive option possible
- children should have the least possible segregation from their family, friends, community and school
- appropriate education should be given to all children in hospital

Mental Health Act or the Children Act

When dealing with young people under the age of 18, the suitability of the Children Act as opposed to the Mental Health Act should be considered. The Code of Practice states:

'*There is no minimum age limit for detention in hospital under the Mental Health Act. It may be used to detain children or young people where that is justified by the risk posed by their mental disorder and all the relevant criteria are met. However, where the child or young person with a mental disorder needs to be detained, but the primary purpose is not to provide medical treatment for mental disorder, consideration should be given to using Section 25 of the Children Act 1989'.*

Gillick competence (also known as the Fraser guidelines)

A child under 16 is considered competent if they have sufficient understanding and intelligence to enable them to understand fully what is involved in a proposed intervention.

(The case of *Gillick v West Norfolk and Wisbech Area Health Authority and Another* [1986] AC and further developed by the case of Re: R [1992] 1 FLR 190)

Informal admission to hospital and consent to treatment

<u>Children under 16</u>

A Gillick competent child may consent to hospital admission and may be admitted on the basis of that consent. A Gillick competent child may also consent to treatment.

If the child refuses to consent, a parent (or a person with parental responsibility) may override the refusal of a Gillick competent child. However, the Code of Practice advises against this and the application of the Mental Health Act may be more appropriate.

Parental responsibility

It is crucial to understand who holds parental responsibility when providing care or treatment to children. It will usually be the child's parent(s) but, this is not necessarily the case. Where parental responsibility has been granted to a person through a court order, a copy of this should be taken and retained by the hospital. Care or treatment may be authorised by either parent, where a child is not competent to consent to it themselves. However, wherever possible, both parents should be involved. In the event of a dispute between them, authority from the court may be sought.

<u>Children looked after by the local authority (Section 22 of the Children Act 1989)</u>

If children are looked after by social services, treatment decisions should be discussed with a parent or a person with parental responsibility.

<u>Children voluntarily accommodated by the local authority</u>

The rights of the person with parental responsibility remain the same as in other circumstances.

<u>Children subject to a care order</u>

In this situation, parental responsibility is shared between the parents and the local authority and consequently, it is a matter to be agreed between the two parties. The local authority has powers under the Children Act to limit parental responsibility if needed.

When should the court be involved?

A court's decision-making powers may need to be sought when:

> treatment decisions need to be made in relation to a child who is not Gillick competent
> **and**
> the person with parental responsibility cannot be identified
> **or**
> the person with parental responsibility is incapacitated
> **or**
> if the person with parental responsibility does not appear to be acting in the best interests of the child when making treatment decisions for them
> **or**
> there is a dispute between those with parental responsibility

When making decisions for a child, weight should be given to the child's refusal to be treated in proportion with their age and maturity.

Relevant legislation

The Code of Practice states that those responsible for the care of children in hospital should be aware of the following relevant legislation:

- The Children Acts 1989 and 2004
- The Family Law Reform Act 1969
- The Mental Capacity Act 2005
- The Human Rights Act 1988
- United Nations Convention on the Rights of the Child
- Relevant case law

Further information

It will be noted from the above that the care and treatment of children and young people is a complex area and further reading is recommended. The Code of Practice to the Mental Health Act provides detailed information on the issue. The Mental Health Act Commission/Care Quality Commission has produced a guidance note on detaining children (see page 148). Further information about Gillick competence (also known as the Fraser Guidelines) is available via: *www.dh.gov.uk* (search under *'consent'*).

POST

Section 134 of the Act allows hospitals to withhold post sent by or to detained patients in certain circumstances. There are detailed procedures that apply in the event of post being withheld and any decision to do so may be subject to review by the Mental Health Act Commission/Care Quality Commission.

Legal criteria

A patient's out-going post may be withheld if:

it is addressed to a person who has stated they no longer wish
to receive post from the patient

or

the patient is at a high security hospital **and** it is considered that the post
is likely to cause distress to the addressee or to any other person
(this does not apply to members of hospital staff)

or

the patient is at a high security hospital **and** the post is likely
to cause danger to any person.

Likewise, in-coming post can be withheld from a patient detained in a high security hospital if it is considered to be in the interests of the patient's safety or for the protection of others.

Application

A person can make a request to have post withheld from them by writing to either the hospital, the responsible clinician in charge of the patient's treatment or the Secretary of State for Health.

Exceptions

Some organisations and persons are exempt from the above rules. That is, post can neither be stopped going to them nor being delivered from them. They include:

- Members of Parliament (House of Commons and House of Lords)
- Masters (Judges) or any other officers of the Court of Protection
- The Parliamentary and Health Service Ombudsman
- Mental Health Review Tribunal
- NHS organisations
- Local authorities (social services)
- A legal representative of the patient
- Patient advice and liaison service (PALS)
- Independent mental health advocates (IMHA)

Inspection and record keeping

Full details on the procedure for inspecting and retaining post are given in the *Reference Guide to the Mental Health Act* [4]. The Code states that if post has been withheld this must be recorded in writing by an officer authorised by the hospital managers, and the patient must be informed in accordance with the regulations.

NATIONAL ASSISTANCE ACT 1948

Section 47 of the National Assistance Act 1948 provides for the compulsory admission of a person to a hospital or care home who may not necessarily have a mental disorder but needs assistance in looking after themselves.

Section 47 criteria

An application may be made to a Magistrates' Court by the local authority (social services) on the following grounds:

The person is suffering from a grave chronic disease
or
the person is elderly or physically incapacitated and is living in insanitary conditions
and they are unable to look after themselves
or are not being given proper care and attention by others
and
it is necessary to remove the person from their place of residence either in their own interests or to prevent injury or serious nuisance to others.

A doctor must make a written report or give oral evidence to the court confirming the criteria above.

Limitations and duration

➢ Although the National Assistance Act allows admission, it does not permit treatment to be given to a person without their consent.

➢ The initial period of detention is three months, which can be extended by further orders of the court.

After six weeks has passed from the start of the order under Section 47, the person subject to the order (or someone on their behalf) may apply to the court to end it.

VOTING

The Representation of the People Act 2000 allowed the use of a mental health hospital address for the purposes of registering to vote. This has enabled both voluntary (informal) patients and some detained patients to vote.

In order to register to vote, patients can use their own address, an address to which they have a local connection or the address at which they are an in-patient.

If the person is a voluntary patient but unable to leave the ward to vote in person, they can arrange to vote by proxy or make an application for postal voting. A detained patient can only vote by proxy or by post. People detained under a forensic (court/prison related) section of the Act cannot vote.

Further information

The Mental Health Act Commission/Care Quality Commission has produced a guidance note on voting (see page 148).

The following case studies give examples of the Act in practice.

Case study 1: General application of the Act

Julie is in a supermarket when she starts to have delusions and because of her behaviour the police are called. PC Nancoo arrives and tries to calm her down but then suspects that she may be suffering from a mental disorder. PC Nancoo assesses that Julie needs immediate care or control and for the protection of herself or others needs to be removed to a place of safety for assessment.

In this situation the following process could be instigated under the Act:

> ➢ PC Nancoo's assessment of the situation means that she has the power to take Julie to a place of safety (hospital in this case) for assessment (Section 136).
> ➢ Julie arrives at hospital and is assessed the following day. Two doctors (one of them Section 12 approved or approved clinician status) and an approved mental health professional assess Julie and she is detained under Section 2. Section 2 is considered appropriate to assess Julie because this is her first encounter with mental health services.
> ➢ After three weeks under Section 2, it is concluded that Julie has a *mental disorder of a nature or degree that requires treatment in hospital for her own safety*. Due to the assessment period, staff also believe there to be appropriate treatment available for Julie. Following another assessment by two doctors (one Section 12 approved or approved clinician status) and an approved mental health professional, Julie is detained under Section 3.
> ➢ Whilst on Section 3, Julie decides to appeal against her detention and makes an appeal to the Mental Health Review Tribunal. The hearing takes six weeks to arrange and Julie is unsuccessful as the Tribunal is not satisfied that she meets the criteria for discharge.
> ➢ Three weeks later, Julie wishes to appeal again and contacts her solicitor who advises her that as she has already appealed to the Tribunal during this period of detention (the first six months of a Section 3) she cannot do so again. However, he also advises her that she has a right of appeal to the Hospital Managers. Julie instructs her solicitor to appeal on her behalf.
> ➢ At the Hospital Managers' hearing, three weeks later, Julie is discharged.

Case study 2: Appeals and discharge criteria

Sarah is detained under Section 3 of the Act and decides to appeal to the Mental Health Review Tribunal. She has appealed once already to the Tribunal in her last period of detention. However, she is able to appeal to the Tribunal again now her Section 3 has been renewed for a second six month period.

The medical and social circumstances reports for the Tribunal are, on the whole, positive about Sarah's condition. During the Tribunal hearing her solicitor, Mr James, establishes that although she has a mental disorder it is not of a nature or degree that warrants detention in hospital. However, the responsible clinician Dr Lahmar states that she is a risk to her own health and safety. When cross examined on this point, Dr Lahmar states she is a risk to her own health or safety because she has a broken leg which needs time to heal. He states that this is why it is necessary to keep her in hospital as she is unwilling to wait to see a physiotherapist and he fears that she may cause her leg more damage if she is discharged before an assessment is arranged.

Sarah is discharged as the Tribunal are satisfied that she meets the discharge criteria. Although she is suffering from a mental disorder, it is not of a nature or a degree to detain her in hospital. They make it clear that her broken leg is not a mental disorder and consequently, as she has capacity, she cannot be detained to wait for a physiotherapy assessment even though staff may consider this to be in her best medical interests.

Case study 3: Nurse's holding power

Irene is a voluntary (informal) patient. However, staff have become increasingly concerned about her mental health particularly because Irene has said several times that she wishes to leave the ward.

Tracy, a ward nurse, is leaving the ward. Before she is able to close the door behind her, Irene manages to push her way out.

Tracy is a nurse qualified to the Nursing and Midwifery Council level of registered nurse and decides that the circumstances necessitate her using her holding power under Section 5(4) to stop Irene and return her to the ward. She realises that there is not enough time to secure the attendance of a doctor or approved clinician to complete a Section 5(2) instead. After Tracy has secured Irene, she immediately bleeps Dr Sagoo. Mindful of the advice given in the Code of Practice, Dr Sagoo ensures she arrives on the ward as soon as possible and certainly no later than six hours after the Section 5(4) was initiated. On arrival, Dr Sagoo assesses Irene and applies Section 5(2) instead.

Case study 4: Interaction with the Mental Capacity Act

Jim is a voluntary (informal) patient on the older person's mental health ward. He lacks capacity in relation to his finances. Following assessment, the junior doctor tells him that he needs a hip replacement. Jim is very upset by this news and is adamant that he does not want a hip replacement. Even when he is told about the serious consequences to his mobility should he not have one, he refuses to change his mind.

The junior doctor says that as Jim is on a mental health ward, she and another doctor and an approved mental health professional could detain him under the Mental Health Act so that he could then be forced to have the treatment. However the responsible clinician, Dr Lahmar, points out the following to the junior doctor:

- ✓ Even if Jim was detained, it would not be possible to treat him under the Act as the hip replacement is not treatment for mental disorder.
- ✓ Jim does not have capacity in relation to his finances however, capacity is 'issue specific', so they need to assess Jim's capacity in relation to his decision not to have a hip replacement.
- ✓ Although the Mental Health Act cannot be used, if Jim is found to lack capacity in relation to this issue, the Mental Capacity Act 2005 may be used to make a best interests decision on Jim's behalf to have the hip replacement.

Case study 5: Guardianship

Ingrid has been placed under guardianship by two doctors (one Section 12 approved) and an approved mental health professional. Under the guardianship powers, she has been told the following:

- ➢ She should reside at her mother's home.
- ➢ She should attend appointments with her GP every two weeks.
- ➢ She should take her medication (for mental disorder).

After a few weeks, her GP reports that Ingrid has missed an appointment and her mother reports that she does not reside at home every night and often goes without her medication.

The community mental health team discuss the case. In the meeting, a trainee social worker, Cassie, states that it is easily resolved as they can simply physically force her to attend the GP appointments, take her medication and reside at her mother's home.

She is quickly corrected by her supervisor Aziza who explains the following:

- ✓ Under the powers of guardianship, Ingrid can only be *required* to attend her GP appointments, reside at home and take her medication, she cannot be forced to do so.
- ✓ However, as it is vital for Ingrid's mental health that she takes her medication, Aziza states that an approved mental health professional could apply for Ingrid to be assessed with a view to detaining her in hospital again under Section 3 of the Act so that she may be forced to take her medication.

Case study 6: Removal to hospital of prisoners

Mark has been sent to prison recently on remand from a Magistrates' Court following a charge of theft. After a few days one of the prison officers, Chris, has become concerned because Mark has started talking to himself. Mark now complains to Chris that he cannot sleep at night because of voices in his head. Mark further explains that he is trying to resist the voices' instructions but is concerned he will not be able to do so for much longer.

Chris tells his supervisor who organises Mark's assessment by two doctors. Following assessment, it is agreed that Mark is suffering from *mental disorder of a nature or degree which warrants detention and treatment in hospital and that this treatment is urgent.*

The Ministry of Justice is contacted, and having considered the doctors' recommendations, issue a transfer direction under Section 48 to move Mark from prison to hospital.

Case study 7: Community treatment order

Damien is a very successful business man who has a history of recurring depressive episodes with admissions to hospital. When he is well he often disengages from services and fails to take his medication as prescribed. After a recent period of depression, he is admitted to hospital under Section 3 of the Act. After four weeks, his condition improves and his responsible clinician, Dr Zia considers giving him leave. She initially grants Damien weekend leave of two days. This is very successful and after a further stay on the ward, leave is gradually increased. Damien is then given leave of seven days.

The day before he is due to return, he telephones the ward and explains that he is feeling well and has been taking his medication. However, he requests a further day of leave so he can attend a business meeting. Dr Zia thinks it would be beneficial for Damien to slowly immerse himself back into his work and discusses this with Darshana, Damien's community psychiatric nurse. Darshana reminds Dr Zia that if she does grant the additional day, it would be a total of more than seven consecutive days and accordingly, she must first consider whether to discharge Damien subject to a community treatment order.

Dr Zia considers the rules in relation to community treatment orders. She is of the opinion that Damien is sufficiently well that as long as she has a power of recall, he would not be a risk to himself or others if she discharged him subject to a community treatment order. She also considers that he is more likely to take medication in the community if subject to a community treatment order. She knows that Darshana will visit Damien and if there are any concerns, Dr Zia may exercise the power of recall available under the order. She decides to discharge Damien subject to a community treatment order, believing this to be particularly beneficial as it will allow Damien to go back to his daily routine and further improve his mental health.

REFERENCES

1. Commission for Healthcare Audit and Inspection (2007) *Count Me In 2007, Results of the 2007 national census of in-patients in mental health and learning disability services in England and Wales.* ISBN: 978-1-84562-165-0.

2. The Information Centre (2007) *In-patients formally detained in hospitals under the Mental Health Act 1983 and other legislation, NHS Trusts, Care Trusts, Primary Care Trusts and Independent Hospitals, England 1996-7 to 2006-07.* ISBN: 1-84636-180-7. Used with the permission of the Information Centre. Copyright © 2008. All rights reserved.

3. The Information Centre *(2007) Guardianship under the Mental Health Act 1983: England 2007.* Used with the permission of the Information Centre. Copyright © 2008. All rights reserved

4. *Departmen*t of Health and the Welsh Office (2008) *Reference Guide to the Mental Health Act 1983.* Download at www.dh.gov.uk/en/Publicationsandstatistics/index.htm

5. *The* Ministry of Justice (2007) Statistical Bulletin, *Statistics of Mentally Disordered Offenders 2006, England and Wales.*

6. Tribunals Service (2007) *Annual Report and Accounts 2006-2007*

7. Mental Health Act Commission *(2008) Data supplied on request*

8. Department of Health (2008) *Code of Practice, Mental Health Act 1983.* ISBN: 9780113228096

9. Owen G, Richardson G, David A, Szmukler G, Hayward P, Hotopf M et al (2008) *Mental capacity to make decisions on treatment in people admitted to psychiatric hospitals: cross sectional study.* British Medical Journal 337: a448

Mental Health Act 2007 – Further information

At the time of writing (September 2008) the following sources of information are available concerning the changes being introduced by the Mental Health Act 2007.

Website: *www.mhact.csip.org.uk*

To request a monthly newsletter email: *mhact.update@csip.org.uk*

Regional implementation leads

North East	Bruce.Bradshaw@nimheneyh.nhs.uk	07940 361335
North West	Dave Eldon	0161 3514926
East Midlands	Robert Nisbet	07901 670070
Eastern	Lou.Brewster@csip.org.uk	07717 576822
South East	Keithnieland@aol.com	07711 980057
London	Sarah.Haspel@londondevelopmentcentre.org	0207 3072431
South West	David.Pennington@nimhesw.nhs.uk	07799 627244
West Midlands	Colin.Vines@csip.org.uk	07748 703687

Mental Health Legislation Team
Department of Health, Wellington House, 133-155 Waterloo Road, London SE1 8UG

Tel: 0207 972 4477   Email: mentalhealthact2007@dh.gsi.gov.uk

Mental Health Act - Statutory Forms

Form	Use	Section
A1	Application by nearest relative	Section 2
A2	Application by an approved mental health professional	Section 2
A3	Joint medical recommendation	Section 2
A4	Single medical recommendation	Section 2
A5	Application by nearest relative	Section 3
A6	Application by an approved mental health professional	Section 3
A7	Joint medical recommendation	Section 3
A8	Single medical recommendation	Section 3
A9	Emergency application by nearest relative	Section 4
A10	Application by an approved mental health professional	Section 4
A11	Medical recommendation for emergency admission	Section 4
H1	Approved clinician report on hospital in-patient	Section 5(2)
H2	Nurse's holding power	Section 5(4)
H3	Sections 2, 3, and 4 – record of detention in hospital	Section 2, 3, 4
H4	Transfer between hospitals with different managers	Transfer
H5	Renewal of authority for detention	Renewal
H6	Return after more than 28 days AWOL	AWOL
G1	Application by nearest relative	Guardianship
G2	Application by an approved mental health professional	Guardianship
G3	Joint medical recommendation	Guardianship
G4	Single medical recommendation	Guardianship
G5	Record of acceptance of guardianship application	Guardianship
G6	Authority for transfer from hospital to guardianship	Guardianship
G7	Transfer from one guardian to another	Guardianship
G8	Transfer from guardianship to hospital	Guardianship
G9	Renewal of authority for guardianship	Guardianship
G10	Return after more than 28 days AWOL	Guardianship
M1	Reception of a patient in England	Transfer
M2	Report barring discharge by nearest relative	Barring discharge
T1	Section 57 – certificate of consent to treatment and second opinion	Treatment
T2	Section 58(3)(a) – certificate of consent to treatment	Treatment

T3	Section 58(3)(b) – certificate of second opinion	Treatment
T4	Section 58A(3) – certificate of consent to treatment (patients at least 18 years old)	Treatment
T5	Section 58A(4) – certificate of consent to treatment and second opinion (patients under 18)	Treatment
T6	Section 58A(5) – certificate of second opinion (patients who lack capacity to treatment)	Treatment
CTO1	Community treatment order	CTO
CTO2	Change of conditions of a community treatment order	CTO
CTO3	Notice of recall to hospital	CTO
CTO4	Record of patient's detention in hospital after recall	CTO
CTO5	Revocation of community treatment order	CTO
CTO6	Transfer of recalled community patient to a hospital under different managers	CTO
CTO7	Report extending community treatment period	CTO
CTO8	Return after being AWOL for more than 28 days	CTO
CTO9	Community patients transferred to England	CTO
CTO10	Assignment of responsibility for community patients to a hospital under different managers	CTO
CTO11	Certificate of appropriateness of treatment to be given to community patient ("Part 4A certificate")	CTO

Mental Health Act Commission/Care Quality Commission – Information Leaflets
(available from *www.mhac.org.uk*)

General Information Leaflet (available in several languages and easy read)
Information on neurosurgery

Mental Health Act Commission/Care Quality Commission – Guidance Notes
(available from *www.mhac.org.uk*)

Subject	Title
Code	Status of the Code of Practice following the House of Lords' Munjaz ruling
Medication	The RCPsych consensus statement on high dose antipsychotic medicine
Seclusion	Guidance for commissioners on monitoring the use of seclusion
Voting	Voting and detained patients
Children	Children and minors
Anorexia	Guidance on the treatment of anorexia nervosa
Clozapine	Guidance on the administration of clozapine and other treatments
Hospitals	Use of the Act in general hospitals without a psychiatric unit
GPs	General practitioners and the Act
Private care	Issues relating to the administration of the Act in independent hospitals
Leave/Transfer	Issues surrounding Sections 17, 18 and 19 of the Act
Nurses	Nurses, the administration of medication for mental disorder and the Act
Treatment	Guidance for RMOs following the PS case
Treatment	Guidance for RMOs: R v Dr Feggetter and the MHAC
SOADs	People with nursing qualifications and consultation with the other professional in second opinions under the Act
SOADs	Guidance for SOADs: R v Dr Feggetter and the MHAC
Forms	Scrutinising and rectifying forms for admission under the Act
Consent	Consent guidance for commissioners
Relative	Nearest relatives of non-UK residents
Relative	Guidance on the rights of nearest relative under the Act

Sections of the Mental Health Act 1983
(note: sections in italics were introduced by the MHA 2007)

Part I		Application of the Act
Section	1	Application of the Act: 'mental disorder'

Part II		Compulsory admission to hospital and guardianship
Section	2	Admission for assessment
	3	Admission for treatment
	4	Emergency admission for assessment
	5	Application for a patient already in hospital
	6	Effect of application for admission
	7	Application for guardianship
	8	Effect of guardianship
	9	Regulations as to guardianship
	10	Transfer of guardianship in case of death, incapacity etc of guardian
	11	General provisions as to applications
	12	General provisions as to medical recommendations
	12A	*Conflicts of interest*
	13	Duty of approved mental health professionals to make applications
	14	Social reports
	15	Errors on forms and their rectification
	16	*Removed by 2007 Act (Reclassification of patients)*
	17	Leave of absence from hospital
	17A	*Community treatment orders*
	17B	*Conditions*
	17C	*Duration of community treatment order*
	17D	*Effect of community treatment order*
	17E	*Power to recall to hospital*
	17F	*Powers in respect of recalled patients*
	17G	*Effect of revoking community treatment order*
	18	Return and readmission of patients absent without leave
	19	Transfer of patients
	19A	*Assignment of responsibility for community patients*
	20	Duration of detention
	20A	*Community treatment period*
	20B	*Effect of expiry of community treatment order*
	21	Special provisions as to patients absent without leave
	21A	*Patients taken into custody or returned within 28 days*
	21B	*Patients taken into custody or returned after more than 28 days*
	22	Special provisions for patients sentenced to imprisonment etc
	23	Discharge of patients
	24	Visiting and examination of patients
	25	Restrictions on discharge by nearest relative
	26	Definition of 'relative' and 'nearest relative'
	27	Children and young persons in care
	28	Nearest relative of minor under guardianship etc
	29	Appointment by court of acting nearest relative
	30	Discharge and variation of orders under Section 29
	31	Applications to the County Court
	32	Regulations that can be made with regard to the Act
	33	Special provisions as to wards of court
	34	Definitions – responsible clinician etc

Part VII	**Management of Property and Affairs**	
	This was removed by the Mental Capacity Act 2005 in April 2007.	
Part VIII	**Miscellaneous**	
Section	114	Approved mental health professionals – approved by local social services authority
	114A	*Approval of courses etc for approved mental health professionals*
	115	Powers of entry and inspection
	116	Welfare of certain hospital patients
	117	After-care
	118	Code of Practice
	119	Payment of medical practitioners under Part 4
	120	General protection of detained patients
	121	Mental Health Act Commission
	122	Provision of pocket money for in-patients in hospital
	123	Transfer to and from special hospitals
	124	Default powers of the Secretary of State
	125	Inquiries
Part IX	**Offences**	
Section	126	Forgery, false statements etc
	127	Ill-treatment of patients
	128	Assisting patients to absent themselves without leave etc
	129	Obstruction
	130	Prosecutions by local authorities
Part X	**Miscellaneous and supplementary**	
Section	*130A*	*Independent mental health advocates*
	130B	*Arrangements under Section 130A*
	130C	*Section 130A: supplemental*
	130D	*Duty to give information about independent mental health advocates*
	131	Informal admission of patients
	131A	*Accommodation etc for children*
	132	Duty of hospitals to give information to detained patients
	132A	*Duty to give information to community patients*
	133	Duty of hospitals to inform nearest relative of discharge
	134	Correspondence of patients
	135	Warrant to search for and remove patients
	136	Police power of arrest
	137	Provisions as to custody, conveyance and detention
	138	Retaking of patients escaping from custody
	139	Protection for acts done in pursuance of the Act
	140	Reception of special cases
	141	Members of Parliament suffering from mental illness
	142	Pay, pensions etc of mentally disordered people
	142A	*Regulations as to approvals in relation to England and Wales*
	142B	*Delegation of powers of managers of NHS foundation trusts*
	143	General provisions as to regulations, order and rules
	144	Power to amend local Acts
	145	Interpretation
	146	Application to Scotland
	147	Application to Northern Ireland
	148	Consequential and transitional provisions and repeals
	149	Short title, commencement and application to Scilly Isles

Schedules (introduced by Mental Health Act 2007)

Download: *www.dh.gov.uk/en/Healthcare/NationalServiceFrameworks/Mentalhealth/ DH_077352*

Schedule 1 — Categories of mental disorder: further amendments etc
        Part 1 — Amendments to 1983 Act
        Part 2 — Amendments to other Acts

Schedule 2 — Approved mental health professionals: further amendments to 1983 Act

Schedule 3 — Supervised community treatment: further amendments to 1983 Act

Schedule 4 — Supervised community treatment: amendments to other Acts

Schedule 5 — Cross-border arrangements
        Part 1 — Amendments to Part 6 of 1983 Act
        Part 2 — Related amendments

Schedule 6 — Victims' rights

Schedule 7 — Mental Capacity Act 2005: new Schedule A1

Schedule 8 — Mental Capacity Act 2005: new Schedule 1A

Schedule 9 — Amendments Section 4A and Schedule A1 to Mental Capacity Act 2005
        Part 1 — Other amendments to Mental Capacity Act 2005
        Part 2 — Amendments to other Acts

Schedule 10 — Transitional provisions and savings

Schedule 11 — Repeals and revocations
        Part 1 — Removal of categories of mental disorder
        Part 2 — Replacement of "treatability" and "care" tests
        Part 3 — Approved clinicians and responsible clinicians
        Part 4 — Safeguards for patients
        Part 5 — Supervised community treatment
        Part 6 — Organisation of Tribunals
        Part 7 — Cross-border arrangements
        Part 8 — Restricted patients
        Part 9 — Miscellaneous
        Part 10 — Deprivation of liberty

Regulations (introduced by Mental Health Act 2007)

Download: *www.dh.gov.uk/en/Healthcare/NationalServiceFrameworks/Mentalhealth/ DH_077359#_13*

- National Health Service Act 2006: Mental Health Act 1983 Approved Clinician (General) Directions 2008

- The Mental Health (Nurses) (England) Order 2008 No.1207

- The Mental Health (Mutual Recognition) Regulations 2008 No.1204

- The Mental Health (Conflicts of interest) (England) Regulations 2008 No.1205

- Mental Health (Approved Mental Health Professionals) (Approval) (England) Regulations 2008 No.1206

Detention criteria

For several sections a number of standard terms are used in the detention criteria that must be met to allow for detention. The meaning of these terms is given below:

Mental disorder

Mental disorder as used in the Act means any *'disorder or disability of the mind'*. The Code of Practice notes that among other conditions this includes:

- affective disorders, such as depression and bipolar disorder
- schizophrenia and delusional disorders
- neurotic, stress-related and somatoform disorders, such as anxiety, phobic disorders, obsessive compulsive disorders, post-traumatic stress disorder and hypochondriacal disorders
- organic mental disorders such as dementia and delirium (however caused)
- personality and behavioural changes caused by brain injury or damage (however acquired)
- personality disorders
- mental and behavioural disorders caused by psychoactive substance use
- eating disorders, non-organic sleep disorders and non-organic sexual disorders
- learning disabilities
- autistic spectrum disorders (including Asperger's syndrome)
- behavioural and emotional disorders of children and adolescents

Learning disability

Although learning disabilities are forms of mental disorder as defined in the Act, for detention under Section 3, 35, 36, 37, 38, 45A, 47, 48, guardianship or a community treatment order the learning disability **must** be *'associated with abnormally aggressive or seriously irresponsible conduct'* for detention to take place *(Section 1(2A))*.

This rule however does not apply to detention under Section 2.

The Code states: *'The learning disability qualification does not apply to autistic spectrum disorders (including Asperger's syndrome). It is possible for someone with an autistic spectrum disorder to meet the criteria for compulsory measures under the Act without having any other form of mental disorder, even if their autistic spectrum disorder is not associated with abnormally aggressive or seriously irresponsible behaviour.'*

Nature or degree

A person can be detained if their mental disorder is either of a *nature or degree* to warrant detention. Both requirements do not have to be satisfied.

The Code states that: *'Nature refers to the particular mental disorder from which the patient is suffering, its chronicity, its prognosis, and the patient's previous response to receiving treatment for the disorder. Degree refers to the current manifestation of the patient's disorder.'*

Appropriate medical treatment is available

The phrase *'appropriate medical treatment is available'* can be split into four components which must all be met.

Appropriate = Medical treatment which is appropriate in the individual patient's case, taking into account the nature and degree of the mental disorder and all other circumstances of their case. This should include consideration of many issues such as the patient's culture, ethnicity, religion, age, gender, family and social relationships as appropriate for the patient concerned. The Code of Practice states that any treatments which require the patient's co-operation to be effective are not inappropriate simply because a patient does not wish to engage with them.

Medical treatment = Medical treatment for mental disorder is defined by the Act (Section 145) and it includes nursing care, psychological intervention and specialist mental health habilitation, rehabilitation and care. This allows a broad range of treatments including medication, care to alleviate the symptoms of the disorder, nursing care, monitoring blood where this is part of taking certain medication, diagnostic tests for mental disorder and the care provided whilst a patient is in seclusion. General medical treatment may also be given if it can be shown to be treating a symptom directly resulting from the patient's mental disorder or integral to it. For example, the use of nasal-gastric tube feeding in the case of a patient with anorexia nervosa.

Treatment = The word treatment is further defined in the Act and means treatment '*the purpose of which is to alleviate or prevent a worsening of, the disorder or one or more of its symptoms or manifestations*'. The Code of Practice notes that '*Medical treatment may be for the purpose of alleviating, or preventing a worsening of, a mental disorder even though it cannot be shown in advance that any particular effect is likely to be achieved.*' Symptoms and manifestations can mean the way a disorder is experienced by the patient and how it manifests itself in the person's thoughts, emotions, communication, behaviour and actions.

Available = The treatment must be available to the patient. It is not sufficient that appropriate treatment could theoretically be provided. The Code states however that, '*...available treatment need not be the most appropriate medical treatment that could ideally be made available. Nor does it need to address every aspect of the person's disorder.*'

Therefore, for a person to be detained under the Act, where the criteria states '*appropriate medical treatment is available*' all four elements above must be satisfied.

Drug and alcohol dependence

Dependence on drugs or alcohol is not classed as a mental disorder within the Act. The Code of Practice states:

'*This means that there are no grounds under the Act for detaining a person in hospital (or using other compulsory measures) on the basis of alcohol or drug dependence alone. Drugs for these purposes may be taken to include solvents and similar substances with a psychoactive effect.*

The Act does not exclude other disorders or disabilities of the mind related to the use of alcohol or drugs. These disorders – for example, withdrawal state with delirium or associated psychotic disorder, acute intoxication and organic mental disorders associated with prolonged abuse of drugs or alcohol – remain mental disorders for the purposes of the Act.

Alcohol or drug dependence may be accompanied by, or associated with, a mental disorder which does fall within the Act's definition. If the relevant criteria are met, it is therefore possible (for example) to detain people who are suffering from mental disorder, even though they are also dependent on alcohol or drugs. This is true even if the mental disorder in question results from the person's alcohol or drug dependence.

Medical treatment for mental disorder under the Act (including treatment with consent) can include measures to address alcohol or drug dependence if that is an appropriate part of treating the mental disorder.'

*   *   *   *   *

Section 12 approved doctor
A doctor who is either also an approved clinician or is Section 12 approved (experience of psychiatry).

Second opinion appointed doctor (SOAD)
A doctor approved by the Mental Health Act Commission to give second opinions as required under the consent to treatment procedures contained in the Act.

Abbreviations

AC   - Approved Clinician
AMHP - Approved Mental Health Professional
CQC   - Care Quality Commission (replacing the Mental Health Act Commission)
CTO   - Community Treatment Orders (Supervised Community Treatment)
ECT   - Electro-convulsive therapy
IMHA   - Independent Mental Health Advocate
MHAC - Mental Health Act Commission
MHRP - Mental Health Review Panel (replacing the Mental Health Review Tribunal)
MHRT - Mental Health Review Tribunal
RC   - Responsible Clinician
SCT   - Supervised Community Treatment (Community Treatment Order)
SOAD - Second Opinion Appointed Doctor